EMMETT MAGAZINE

CONTENTS

ISSUE 1

COVER

CONTENTS

CONTRIBUTORS

CONTACT

ARTISTS – DJ Herbin-Dori Jalazo-Dennis Wells

Krystal Hart-Steven Cozart-Alix Weems-Emmett Williams

FEATURED ARTIST - D J Herbin Interview by Fred Little

SINGER-Vanessa Ferguson by Fred Little

MUSICIAN-Dennis Coffey/Emmett Williams Q & A

FASHION - SherylStyle

ART - Emmett Williams

EVENTS-African American Atelier Annual Members Show

Steven Cozart Featured Artist Q & A with Emmett Williams

PHOTOS – Sheryl M. Williams, Candi Williams Photography

RADIO/FILM - Dee Dee Walker by Emmett Williams

REMEMBERING-Jacquelyn Hughes Mooney by Valerie Jones

ART CLASS - Alix Weems by Raena Mitchell

EDITORIAL - Emmett Williams

CONTRIBUTORS

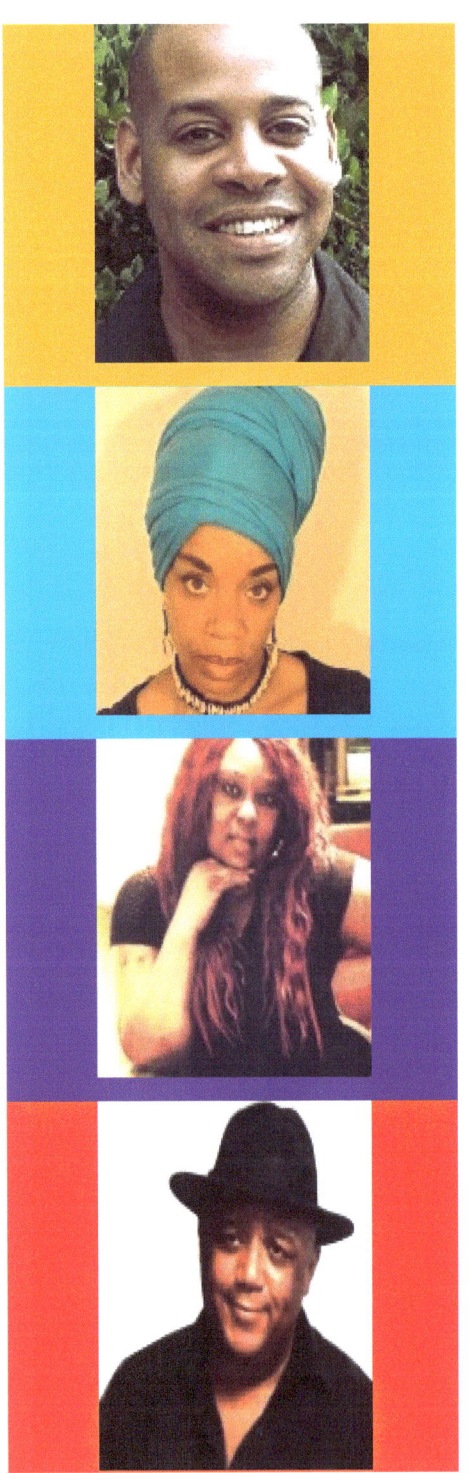

Writer
Editor In Chief

Fred Little is a DC born local Writer in the Greensboro, NC area. For years he has covered local talent in the city and writes for this publication as well, which focuses its coverage on local visual Artists and up and coming performing Artists.

Writer

Queen V Owner of Spot-TV is a Writer, Videographer and Interviewer in Greensboro, NC.

See her written work on notable Quilter/Fiber Artist New Orleans born Jacquelyn Hughes-Mooney.

Fashion
Events Photography

SherylStyle is a Designer and Stylist. Look for her photos and videos here on the Fashion page. Read her personal story on how she became a designer. Sheryl also works on covering events for the magazine.

Art
Publisher
Emmett Williams,
EMMETT MAGAZINE

"I want to interview Artists who have something to say, and give insight into their Art."

D J HERBIN

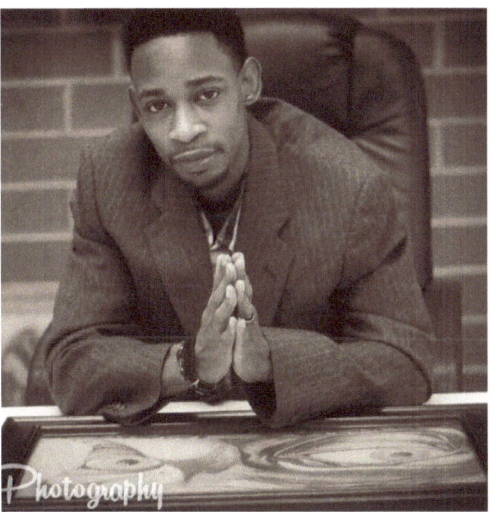

By Fred Little

Squeezing paint out of a tube to create astonishing commissioned portraits Greensboro, North Carolina native and Page High school graduate, (2001), Dwayne Herbin has come a long way from painting Bart Simpson on jeans in Elementary school.

" I was always into the Art grind even as a young boy I painted Marvel characters on lunch boxes, tee shirts, sneakers and even boots for candy money," said Herbin. In years to come he painted more wearable art such as jackets even mannequins for retail stores were added to his arsenal.

Herbin also shows an edgier art side and paints grill tops, vehicle hoods, sculpted steel and metal garage doors at mechanics shops in the Triad and east coast.

As life has peaks and valleys so has Herbin's artistic journey. For approximately 10 years he just worked at a cement company as a laborer. " I almost worked myself to death and my art production suffered," said Herbin. His duties included manually moving cement slabs used for parking and speed bumps. This may have resulted in him developing a rare auto immune illness which affected his motor skills. This ailment made him wheelchair bound and required him to draw disability. But in this valley of life he rediscovered sketching nature.

This lasted for about 6 months and inspired him to name his Art exhibition "Mercy". Herbin feels blessed to have received a second chance and wants his story and Art to inspire others to pursue their dreams and fearlessly display their gifts. "Inspire" may be the next Herbin Exhibition.

Check DJ Herbin on Facebook Twitter and Instagram.

https://www.instagram.com/dherbinart/

This Article Continues on the next page

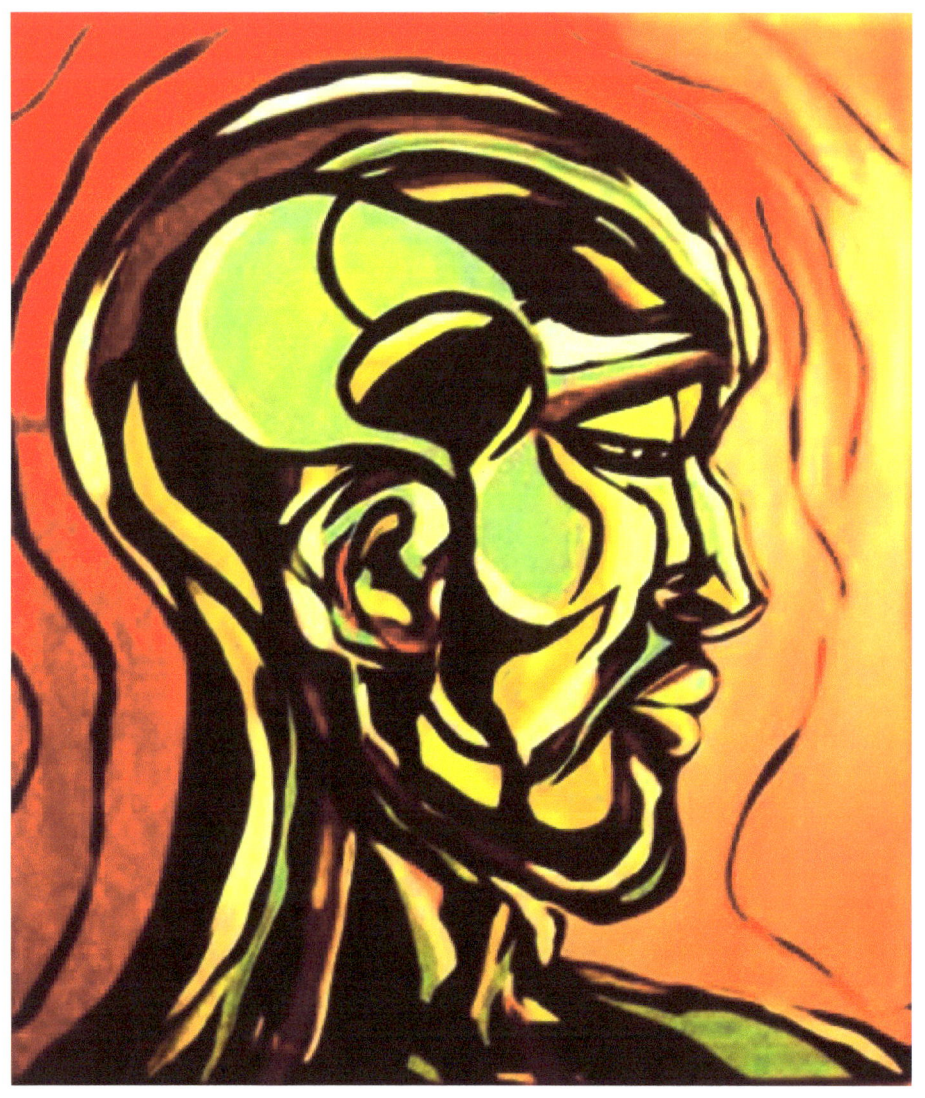

"My natural ability allowed me to see at an early age that I was pretty good. My surroundings inspire me most of all. I was about 7 years old when I really began to sit down and draw a lot. Then at bout 15 years of age, I began to take my talent seriously." The Artist recalls. Herbin has been seen painting live downtown in Greensboro, NC.

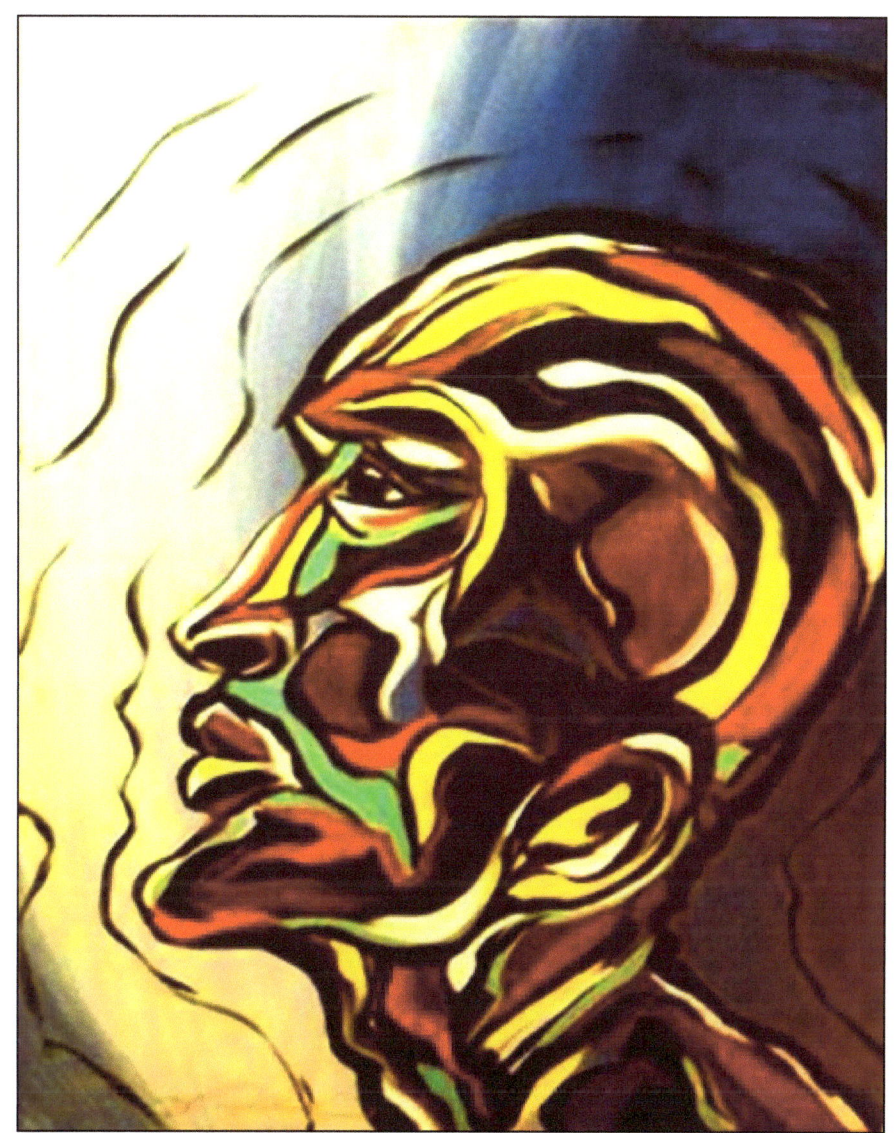

The Artist won a state art contest in 2001 as a student.

Herbin's works have been seen at The African American Atelier, Uptown Artworks, ArtSpace Uptown, The Artist Bloc, local barbershops, diners, coffee shops, clubs, parks and recreation centers. He has also created murals for client's homes in the Triad.

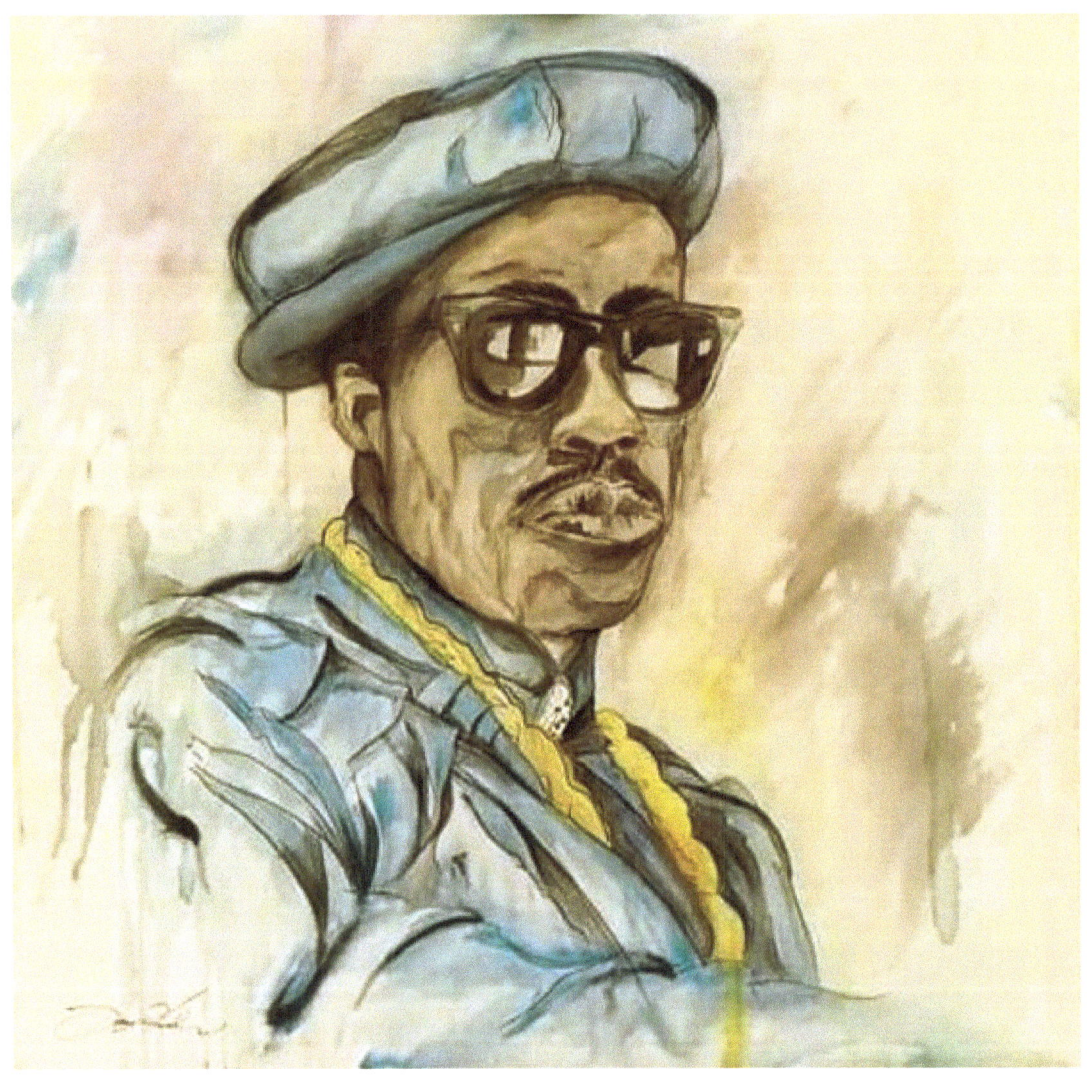

" I use acrylic paint mostly but I have created with Spray paint, pastels, wood, metal, cloth, along with pencil and ink on just about anything that I can get my hands on."

Herbin describes his Art as natural, bold, colorful, and precise.

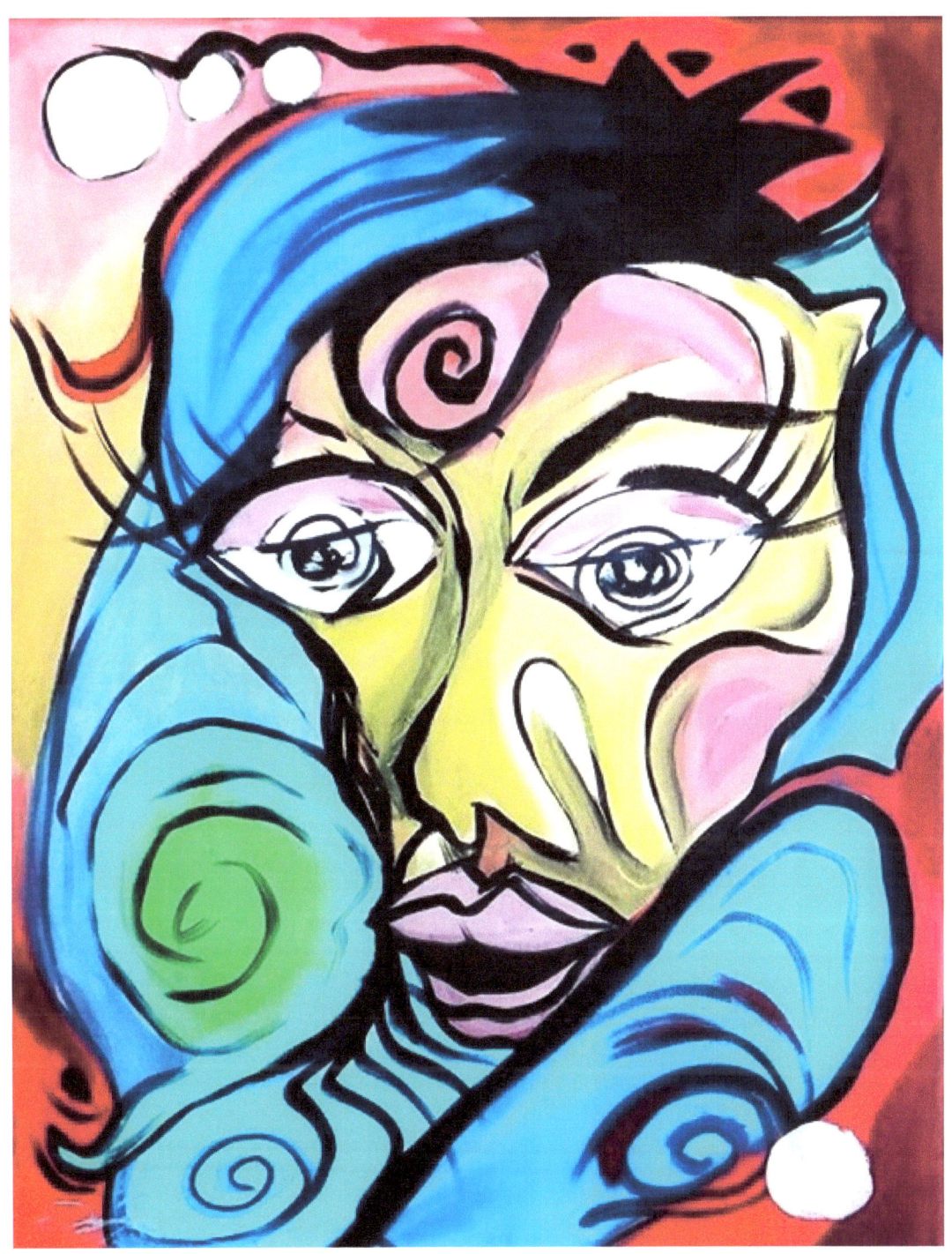

©D J Herbin

Dennis Wells

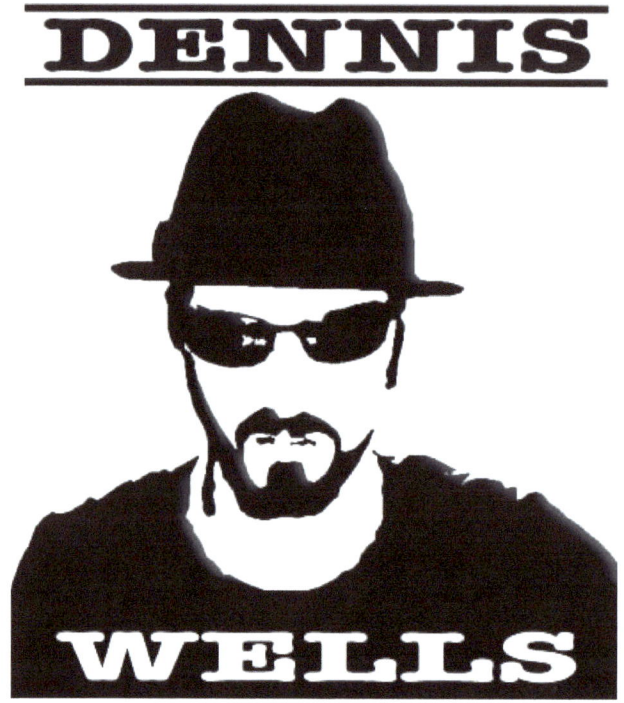

Questions & Answers

Why do you make Art?

I'm not sure that I can or would want to point to any one thing. Creating is almost a compulsion for me. Something I feel like I need to do.

Do you remember when you first began to make Art?

I don't remember a time when I did not love to create. I remember being in elementary school and drawing on the last few feet of paper from blue print rolls my father would bring home from work.   As a full time professional though it has been six years.

How would you describe your Artwork?

I would describe it as contemporary objective abstract with cubist influences or interesting angular interpretation of life.

What is your favorite medium to work with?

I love to try new mediums and techniques so it can vary greatly from piece to piece. The majority of my work is in acrylics and pen and Ink.

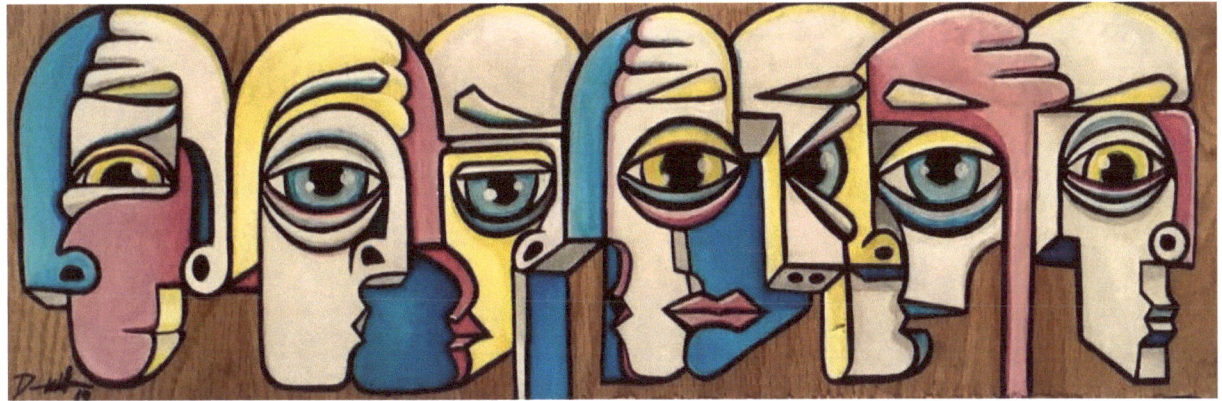

Where can folks find your Artwork?

I'm a member and almost always have a few pieces at Delurk Gallery and Red Dog Gallery in Winston Salem, NC. My work is also available at Modern Furniture Studio in Charlotte, NC, but I have shown in many other cities including Durham, Greensboro, and Los Angeles.

Do you have any current or upcoming exhibitions?

I had two shows in 2019 in Winston Salem and Pasadena in October.

I'm always creating and looking for opportunities and venues but don't have any solo showings on my calendar at the moment.
As for my work, I am hoping to put together a small body of sculptural work for next year.

The Artist's Prices Range from $30 to $3000

Sizes of his works are 4" x 6" up to 4' x 5'

Materials include: Acrylic Paint on Wood Blocks, and Canvases.

https://www.denniswellsartwork.com/public-art

See the public works by Wells in Winston-Salem, North Carolina. "The Chase" and "The Clockwork Kid" are cool sculptural pieces by Dennis Wells, and there are equally impressive murals which include...

"Well Groomed", "Alone with a Memory", "Let the Walls Talk" and "Neighbors" my personal favorite.

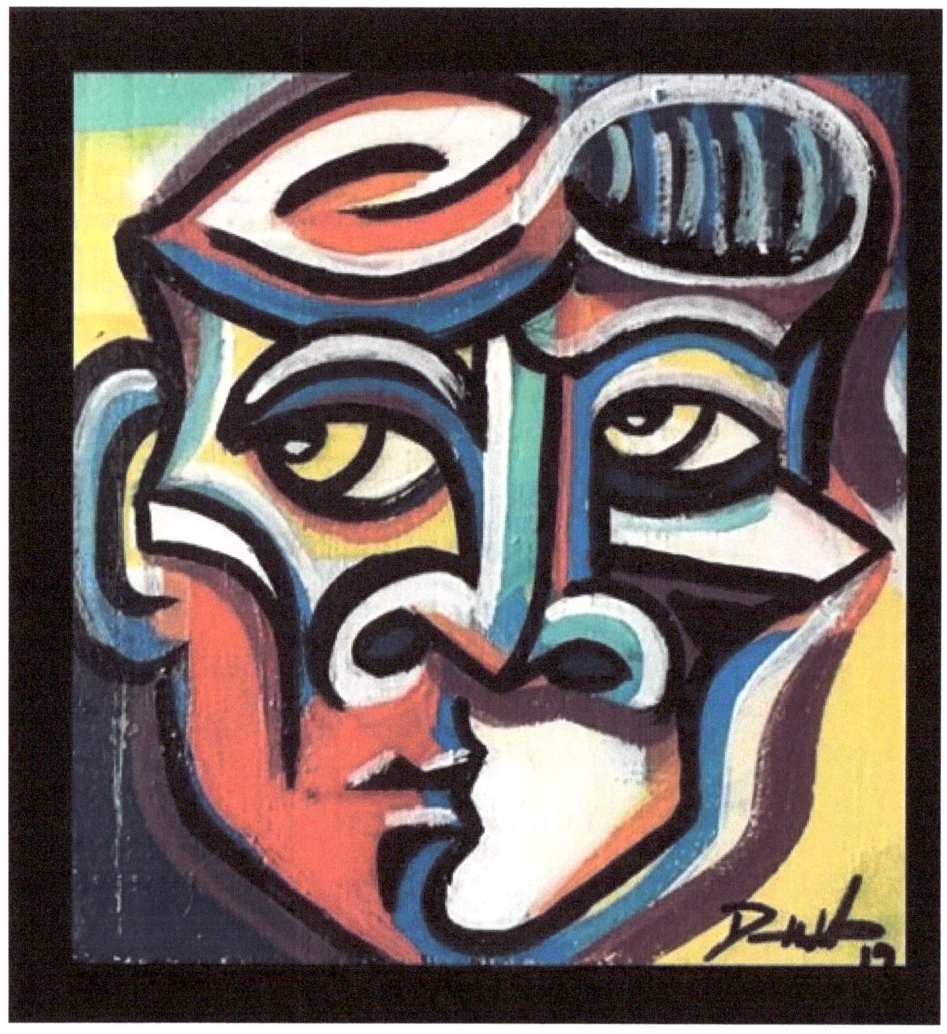

©Dennis Wells

Wells has also supplied his art to the Art-O-Mat system of re-purposed vending machines, which dispense affordable art, instead of cigarettes.

Contact Information
Dennis Wells Art Work In Facebook

Dennis_Wells_Art on Instagram

www.DennisWellsArtWork.com

KRYSTAL HART

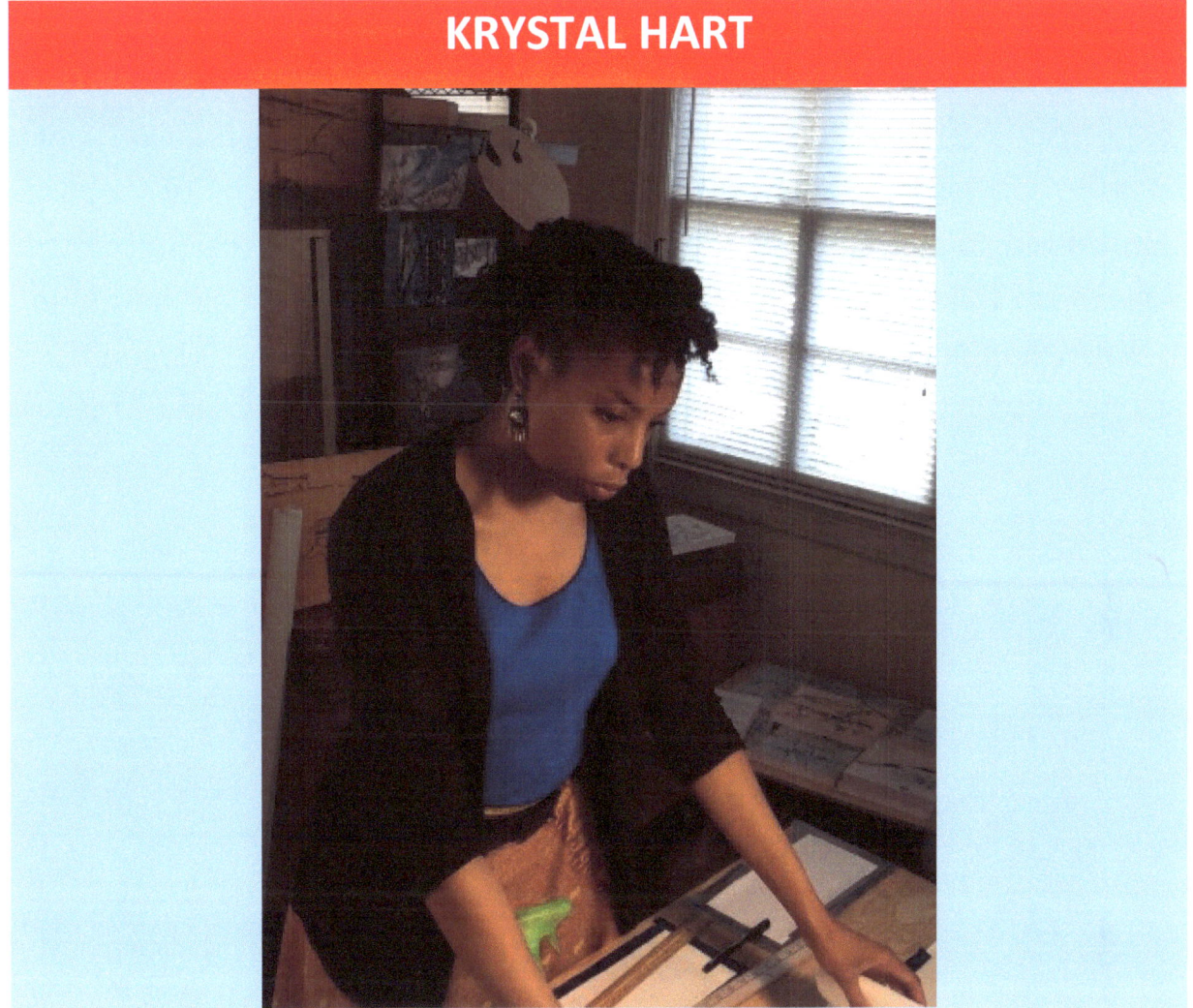

https://www.krystalhart.com/

The Artist describes her Art as Contemporary. The work is constructed from various media including recycled materials.

Hart has traveled to speak with survivors of hurricanes and volunteers her time at cancer centers. Her various and numerous works fall in the category of Abstract Art. She has achieved numerous awards and accolades, as well as being chair on boards. The artist works in North Carolina near her family and its business, and Hart has a mural painted on the building's exterior walls in downtown Greensboro, North Carolina. She feels she is 'compelled to make art', and enjoys the creative process to explore emotive responses. She states she is 'looking for hope in adversity' through her images. Hart studied at The New York Institute of Technology in New York where she received her degree. Hart was selected for a juried show at Atlantic Gallery in NYC. Hart has also participated in Art Basel in Miami through the Hampton Art Lovers Gallery in Miami, Florida. She has an upcoming exhibition in Winston-Salem, North Carolina at the Contemporary Art Museum called "Drawn".

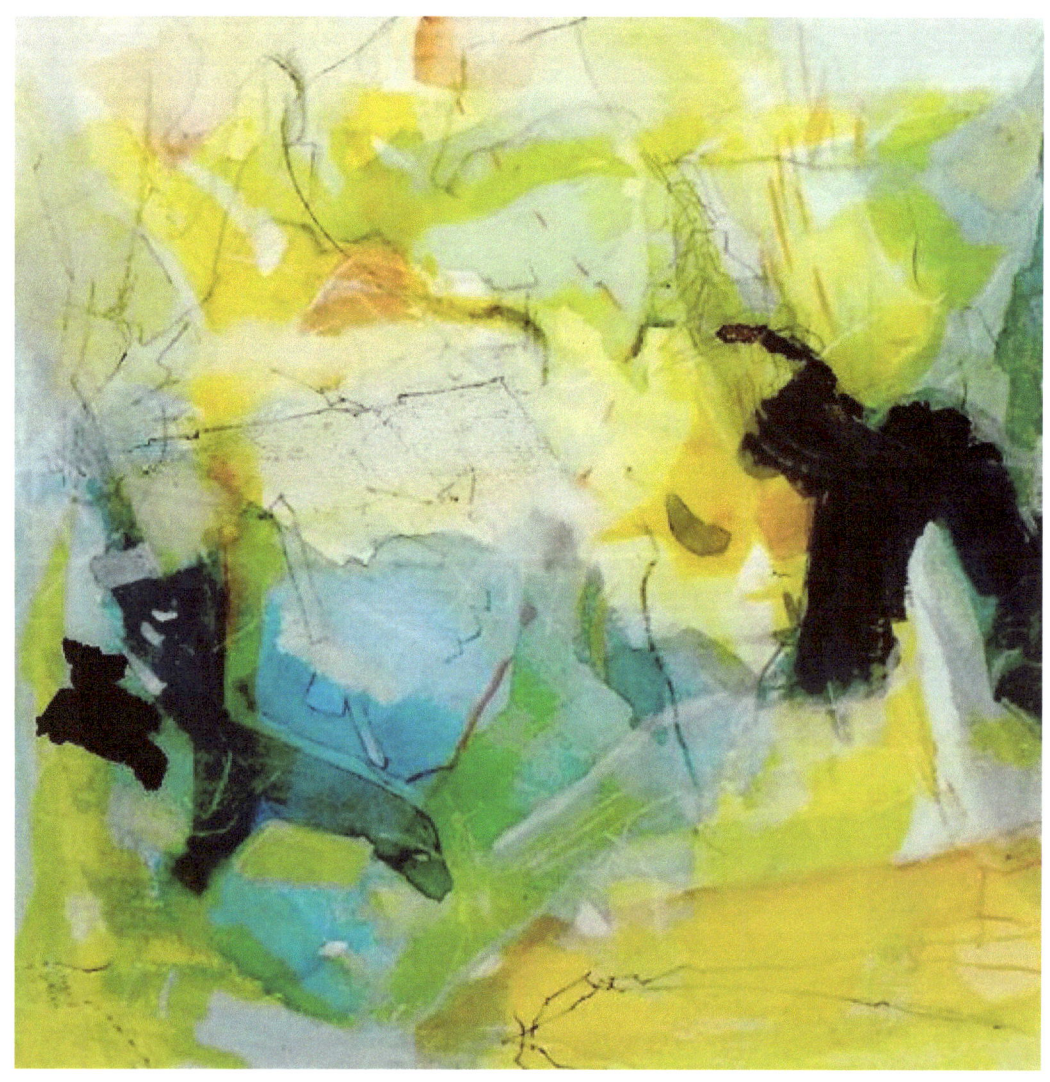

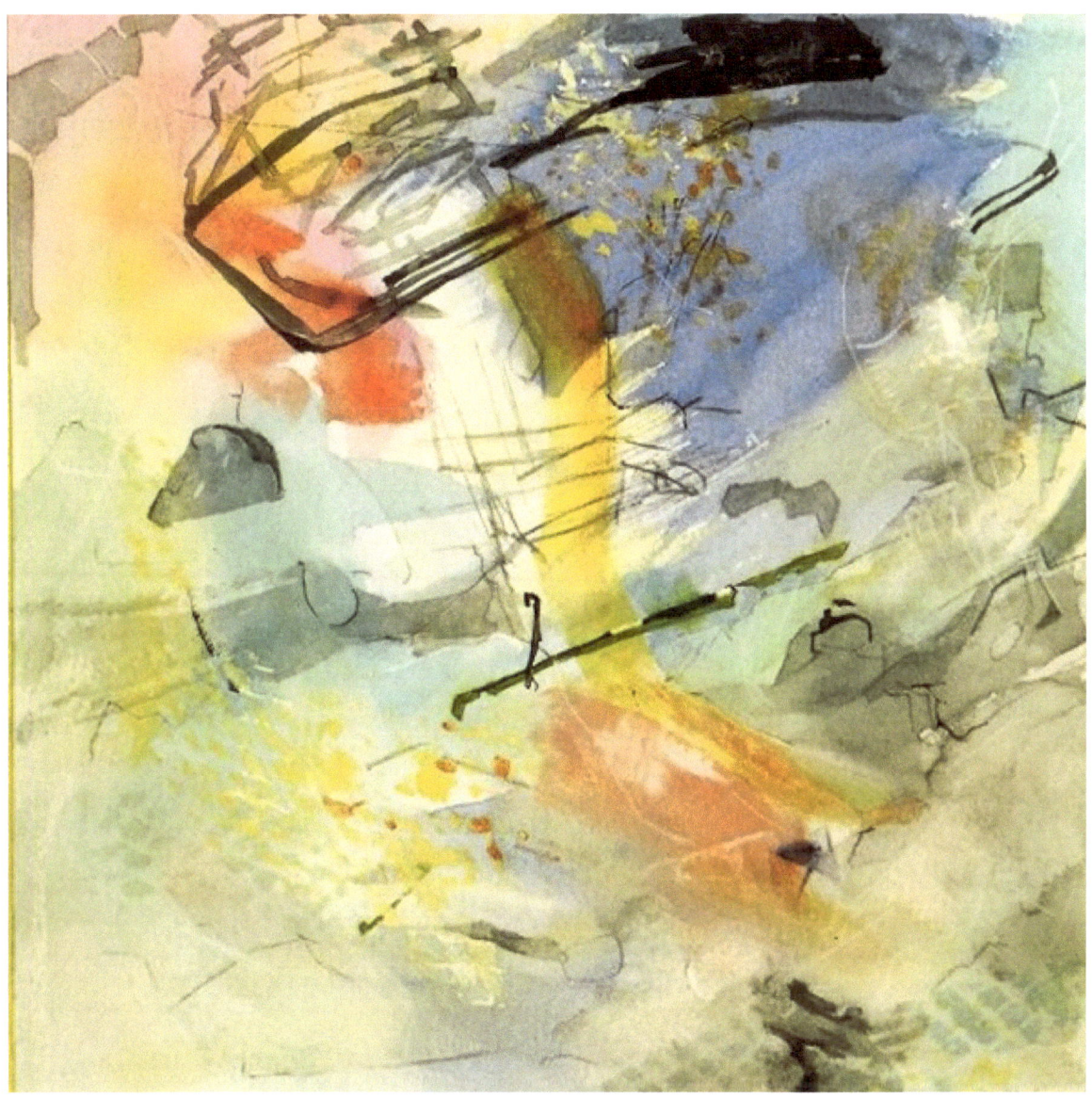

See many more of Hart's art on her Instagram pages.

https://www.instagram.com/artistkrystalhart/

STEVEN COZART

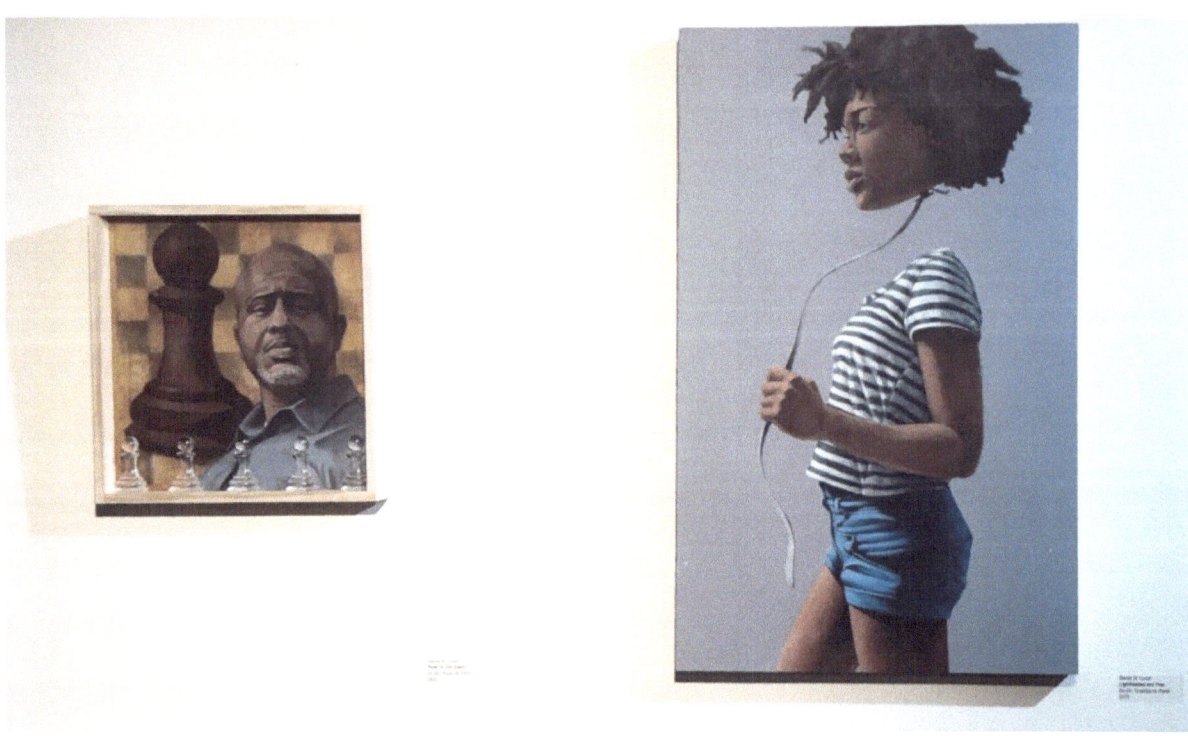

Featured Artist at the African American Atelier 2020

Questions & Answers about his Art and Career

Emmett Williams/Steven Cozart

What inspires you to make Art? What age did you start making Art?

As far back I can remember, I have always been drawing. My earliest memories are of my mother giving me crayons and paper and working with me to draw. I was also following in the footsteps of my older brother, Johnnie, who was a phenomenal artist.

How would you describe your Art?

My work is a type of "stylized realism", using observation to render my subjects (mostly figurative) and adjusting or bending the imagery as I see fit. I introduce other elements, including, mixed media, text, and other objects. A lot of the work/ images that you will see are usually void of environment, which is part of the feel that I have wanted to create as of late.

What materials do you use to make your Art?

I draw and paint, enjoying mixed media. Acrylics are my go-to for painting, as their attributes appeal to me. However, I do enjoy drawing as well, using charcoal, pastel, and graphite. In addition, I will implore different media for effects, which range from inks to instant coffee to collage to resin casts of objects.

Have you exhibited your Art in Galleries and or Museums?

I have had the blessing and opportunity to exhibit in several galleries and museums, including the African American Atelier, Green Hill Center for NC Art, The Greenville Art Museum, the Center for Documentary Studies at Duke University, and the Weatherspoon Art Museum, to name a few.

Do you have any exhibitions coming up or currently?

Currently, I have an exhibition at the Golden Belt Campus in Durham, NC through the Durham Art Guild. Immediately after, I will have several pieces in an exhibition called DRAWN at the South Eastern Center for Contemporary Art (or SECCA) in Winston Salem.

If currently showing, what is your theme of your most recent exhibition?

As of late, my work has begun to reflect my thoughts and feelings about race and identity in America, focusing on stereotypes of the African American Male and Female within the paradigm of the African American Community. This series of drawings, paintings, and mixed media collages refer to the historical practice, in African American communities, of *colorism* and is expanding to include *texturism*.

Do you teach Art? Where, what age groups, and for how long?

I have been a public-school Art Teacher with Guilford County Schools in Greensboro, NC for the last 25 years. I have taught all levels (K – 12) and am currently teaching High School at Weaver Academy for Performing and Visual Art.

Can you offer any tips for beginners? And books you found useful early in life?

In this age, information is readily available through the internet regarding art materials, practice, and skill building. My advice would be to put in the work of self educating, then practice. Stay consistent and work daily, but briefly. Much more is gained by working 30 minutes a day on practicing drawing skills than 3 ½ hours once a week.
Practice should be deliberate. Again, with a little research, it is easy to find instruction online for how to practice fundamentals and experiment with mediums.
WORK IN A SKETCHBOOK. This has saved my practice, as I am busy and cannot always find the time to spend in the studio. The sketchbook has become my mobile studio and has allowed me to investigate and explore ideas so that once I do hit the studio, it is all business.

Regarding books, I would suggest The Illustrator's Bible by Rob Howard. This book contributed to a lot of my studio practice that I still use to this day.

Are there any early inspirational figures in Art, or life?

I gravitated towards Renaissance Art as a child and was taken aback the first time that I saw Caravaggio. Since then, I have come to appreciate and be heavily influenced by artists across several genres, including Basquiat, Henry O. Tanner, hip hop artist Phonte Coleman, writer Jeff Vandermeer , and Jazz Musicians such as Wes Montgomery and John Coltrane.

Do you have any work published in books, or featured in Newspaper, Magazine or Television?

Although I do not have any published works, I do have works from my collection on colorism in the collection at the Rubenstein Library at Duke University.

Contact information, Instagram, Facebook, Website, E-Mail, Address and Phone.

Phone: 336-270-9041 Website: www.stevenmcozart.com Email: merisi39@triad.rr.com
IG: @coz_art_theoneandonly Facebook: https://www.facebook.com/steven.m.cozart/

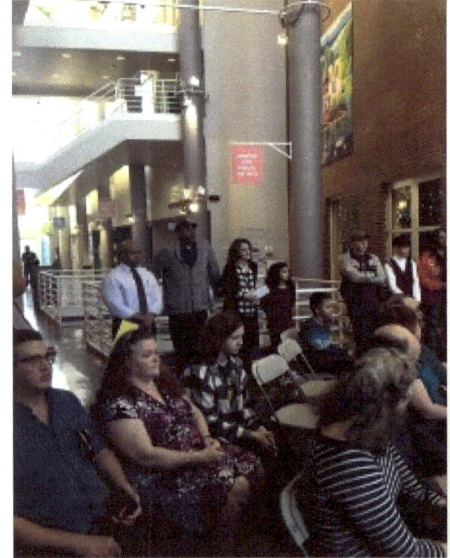
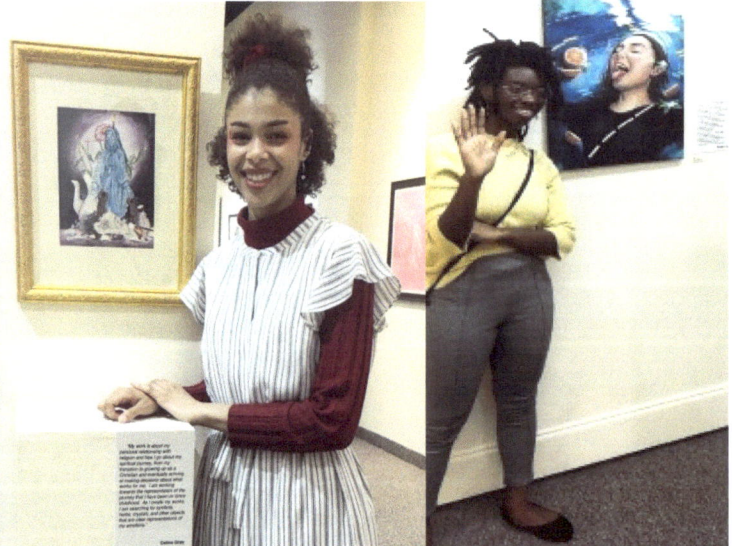

Participating Artists at the African-American Atelier Members Exhibition 2020 in Greensboro, NC.

Photos by Sheryl M. Williams

Alix Weems

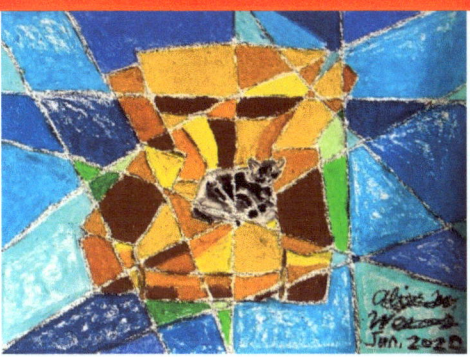

A 29 year old Gifted Talented Artist named Alix Weems was born in state of Baltimore, Maryland.

She's been studying art for over 15 years.

She studied in a variety of mediums including charcoal drawings, colored pencils,

Acrylic paintings and oil pastels to create unique paintings based on realism and abstract art.

She hopes to create even more beautiful artwork to share with the world.

Weems main goal is to progress towards studying oil painting, now that she has familiarity with drawing materials and is confident in her own drawing ability.

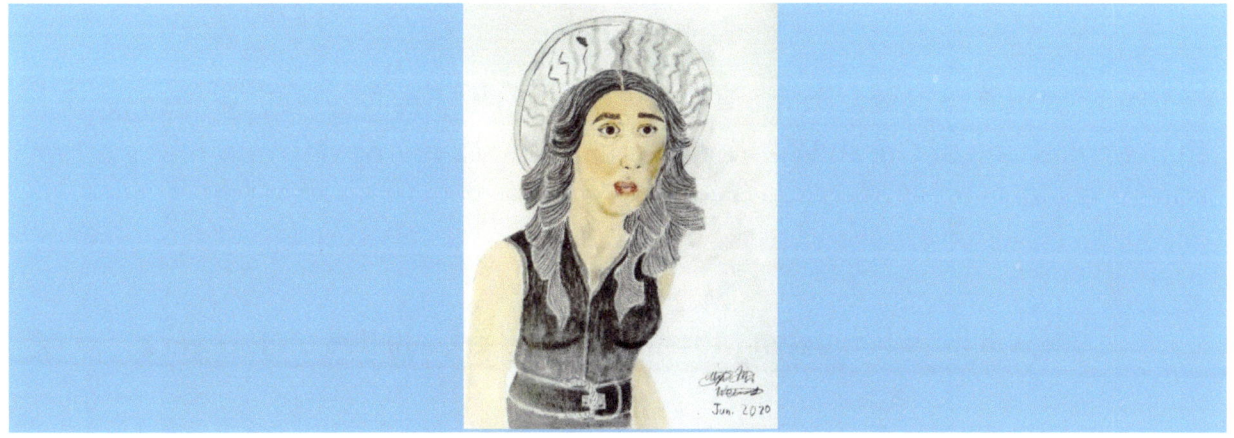

Black Cat on Sofa and Drawing of a Young Woman by Alix Weems.

Contact/Teacher: Raena Mitchell

vision24_7@yahoo.com.

This is for online ZOOM art classes only.

To find out how to register for a session send a message.

Jacquelyn Hughes Mooney

We Remember

Jacquelyn Hughes Mooney

Quilting is an amazing way to preserve history, conserve resources and provide a piece of comfort and for generations to come.

Today I am remembering an artist that came into my life in passing and still has place in my mind and my heart when I think of her work and influence.

Jacquelyn Hughes Mooney, was a wonderful example of living art. Born in New Orleans, in 1950 Mooney's artistic talent carried her throughout the world in fashion, humanitarian acts and in art education

I met Jacquelyn Hughes Mooney in Greensboro, N.C. where she held position at Bennett College for Women as Artist in Residence. It was in 2010 where my fondest memory of Mrs. Mooney was made when she facilitated a quilting workshop at the African American Atelier. The workshop was very well attended by young, old, black and white. What a great way to bring community together.

I encourage you to research more on Jacquelyn Hughes Mooney, whose work is in the collection of Oprah Winfrey, The late Dr. Maya Angelou and many other greats.

We will miss Jacquelyn Mooney but her art will live on forever.

-Queen V

Dori Jalazo

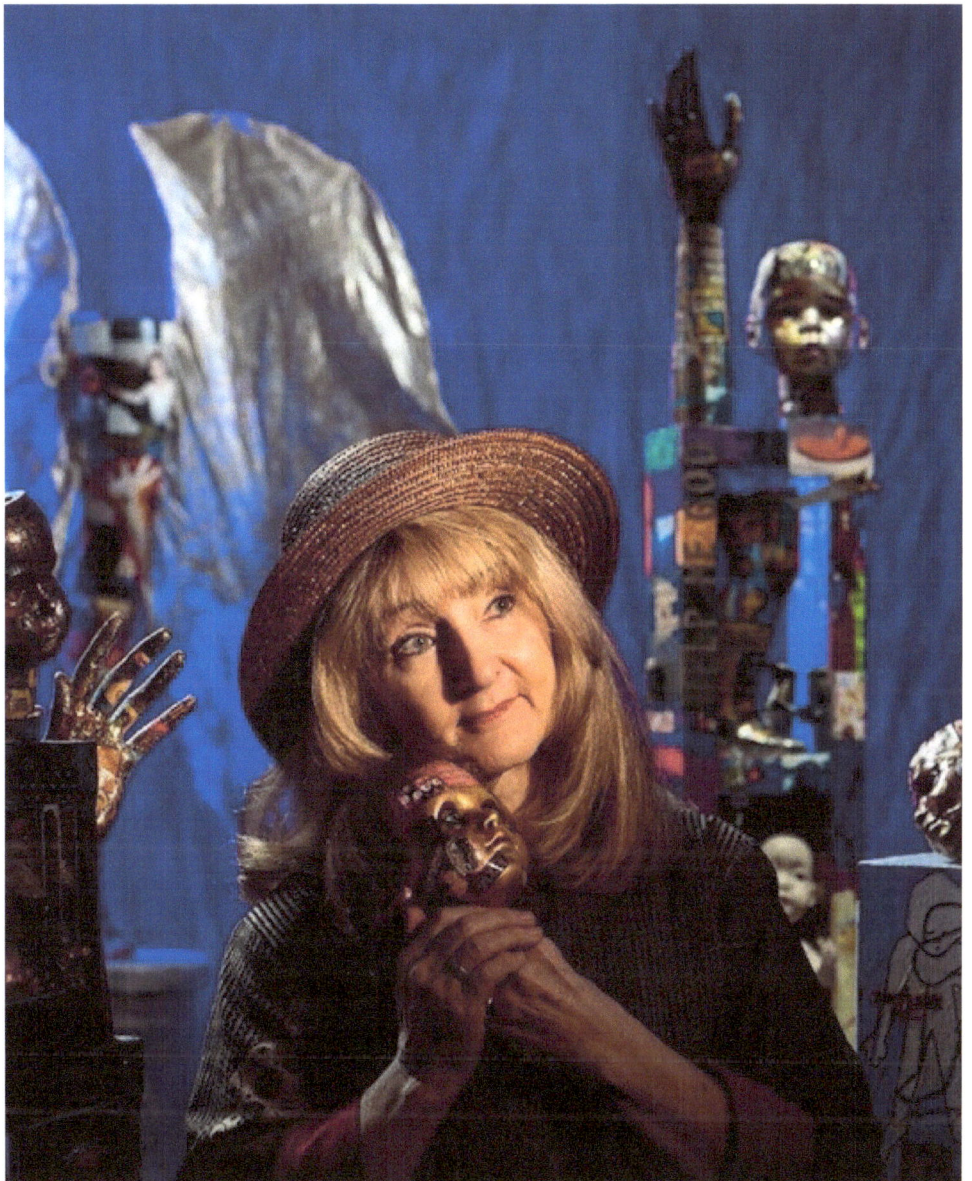

dorij.com

"The Gift that God gave me is me, my own Soul. I have fought hard all my life to give birth to it.
We are all given that gift of our own Soul.
I have to be me, to live my truth, to take responsibility for my mistakes, to help who I can along the way writing, and making Art.
Sometimes it is lonely and hard. I do my best…it's all I've got."
-Dori Jalazo

Jalazo was subjected to severe child abuse as early as age 4 resulting ultimately in

the amputation of a leg.

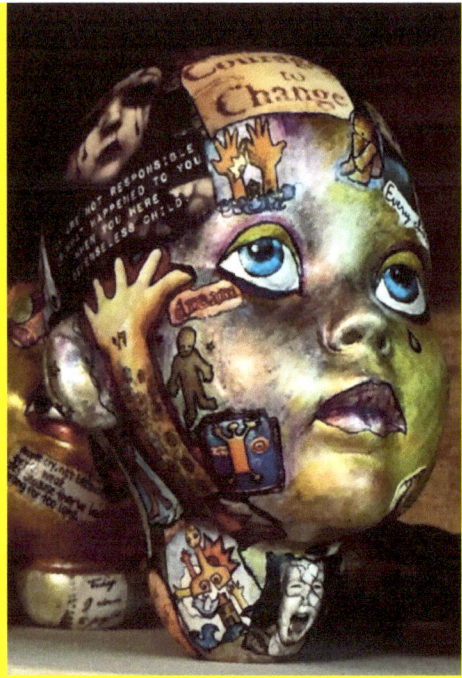

Her mechanism for dealing with the memories of those horrors has been channeled into her Art as means of her only therapy at the time.

On growing into adulthood she has become a master art-maker and speaks to others who can identify with her circumstances, and help them heal as well.

Her installations measure 8 feet around and are in need of a permanent public space.

The installation deals with a variety of imagery and mediums which touch on her memories.

Some of the works in Jalazo's collection have cheerful, whimsical aesthetics.

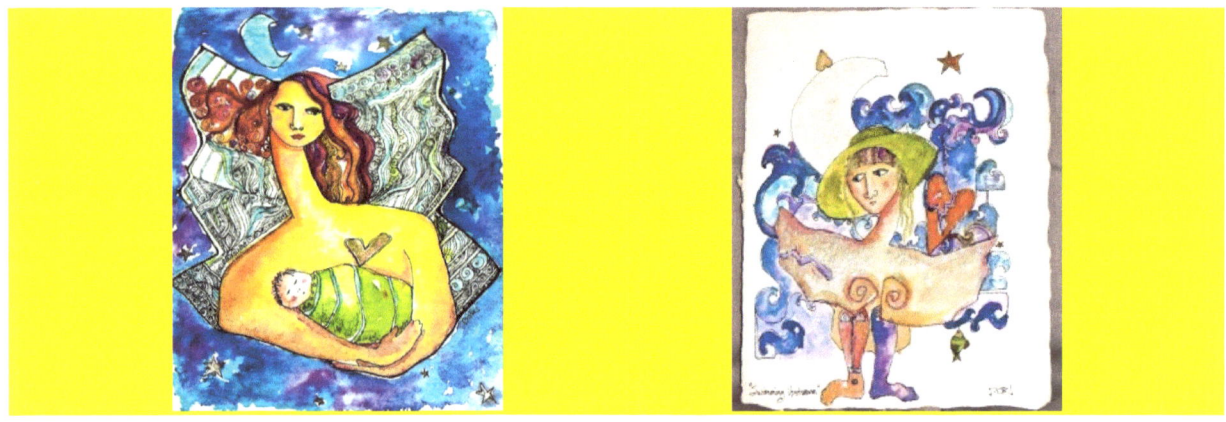

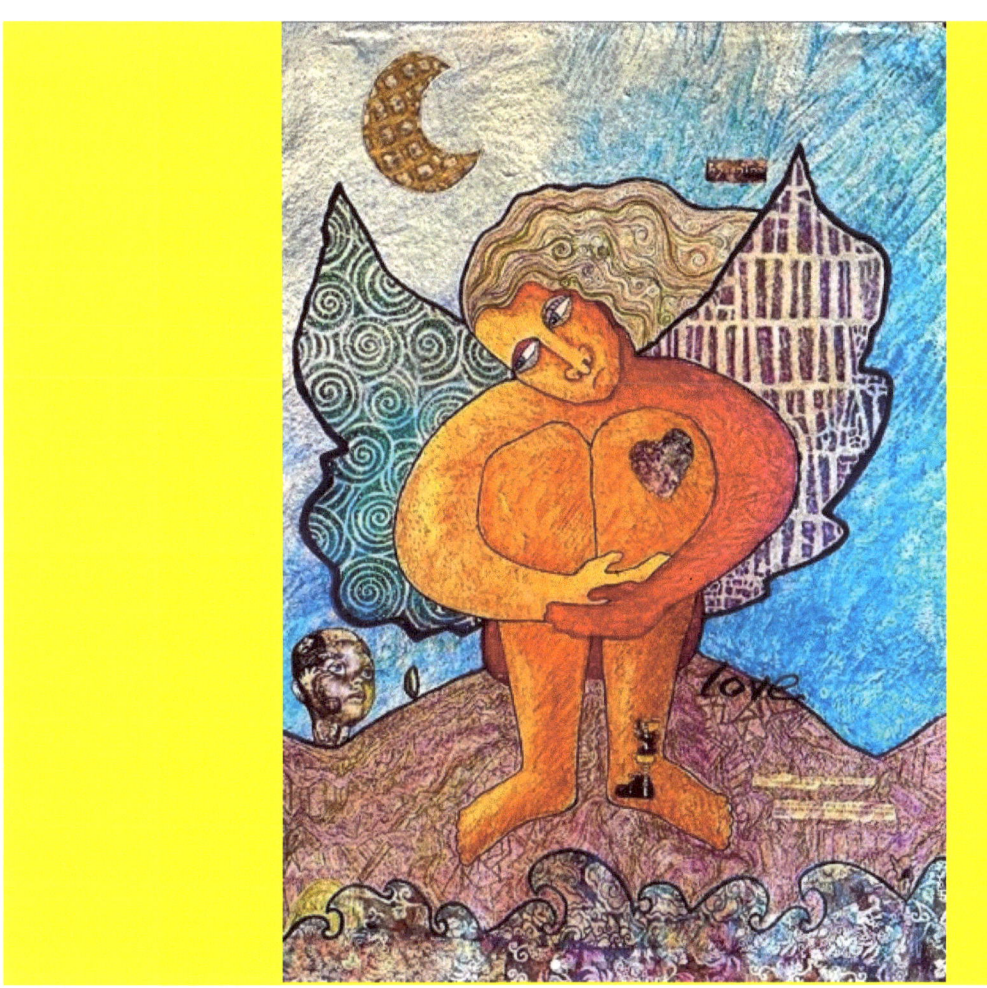

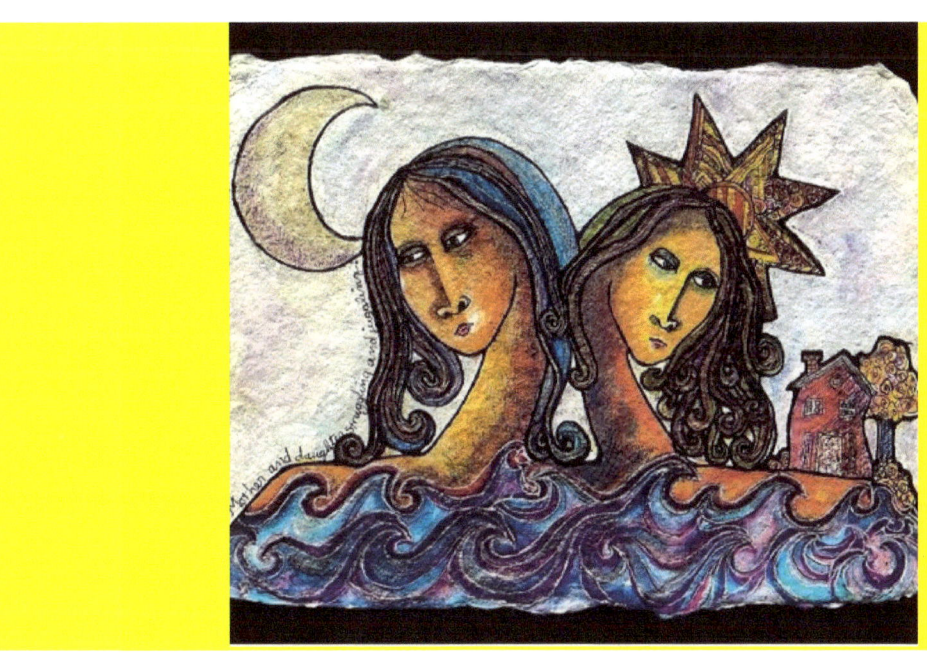

SHERYLSTYLE

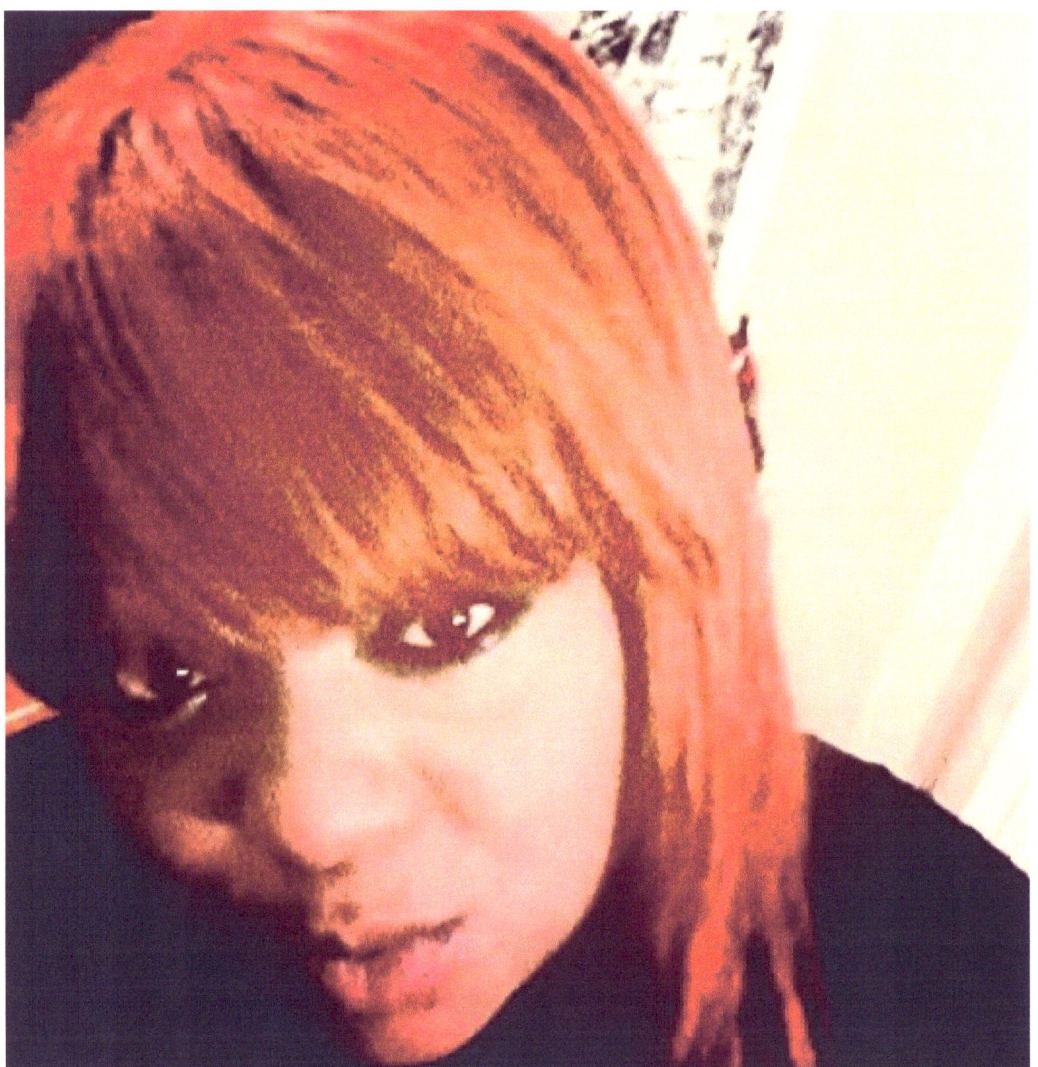

Fashion Designs on the Future

The journey and sacrifice I was willing to make to achieve my dreams I remember was like feeling my insides were on fire. I knew that feeling as a child, it would burn higher when dreaming and drawing and seeing beautiful clothing and accessories.

Then I found a school that seems to have appeared from nowhere. Kingsborough Community College in Brooklyn NY. When I saw this school's fashion program I was drawn in, added perks... it was on Manhattan Beach.

I applied immediately.

I kept telling myself, you are going to be studying fashion on a beach. So when I got the letter of acceptance, I knew that whatever I want in life I have to work toward and believe. I started my fashion education in NY February 28, 2001. It snowed and it was knee high. But for me it seemed like a beautiful spring day. The sun shining bright and so was my future. The fashion department was so professional and I loved everyone who had a desk in there. Theresa Mastrianni who was a faculty member in the retail management program, Darry Romano the creator of the program.

The first time I met the Director of the retail management program, Jacqueline Scerbinski. I immediately noticed her savvy style, she was very classy. I could tell she knew a lot about the fashion industry, and I always valued her teaching in class, paying close attention to her every word, especially when it came to the retail management class. She along with the other professors made a lasting impression on me. I learn so much out there on those waters. Most favorite course, Visual merchandising, TV, Radio and News paper. Sitting in class and the entire class is watching hundreds of commercials, Absorbing advertisements, and Window design, Retail Management, Retail Buying and Business Management.

I realized the Professors were actually individuals who worked in the field and really knew the industry. I valued their expert teaching. I moved to East Orange New Jersey and commuted to Brooklyn NY.

It was challenging. Trains and buses everyday back and forth.

Studies, projects, libraries, exams, up at 4 am to make my 8 am class and getting home in the night.

But that fire was still burning high inside.

One of my fashion instructors was Professor Darry Ramono, who puts on fashion shows every year at the college, where department stores participate by lending clothing for the models to where.

So when he approached my about participating in the show with some of my original designs, first ever having Original designs in the show. I was overwhelmed. And it was such an honor giving his expertise in the field of fashion industry.

I didn't realize that the fashion department was observing me, and believed in me, they stepped in to help me succeed at the show.

I remember crying in the bathroom when I walked in the fashion department and saw needles and thread.

And faculty in the department finishing my hats by hand, steaming my designs coaching me,

And students wanted to wear my designs was emotional.

This confirmation that I am in my journey, I am living my dreams.

That was my very first official fashion show in Brooklyn New York.

And it was the beginning of many to come over the years.

It also gave me the official acknowledgement, I Am a Fashion Designer.

I Am,

SHERYLSTYLE

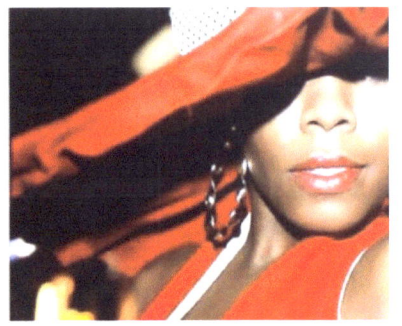
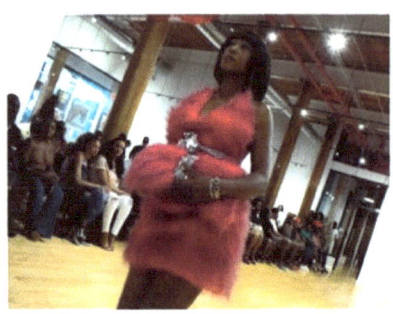
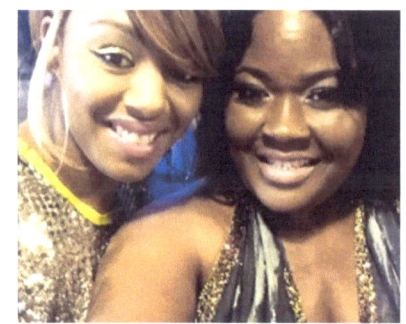

SHERYLSTYLE.com

SHERYLSTYLE

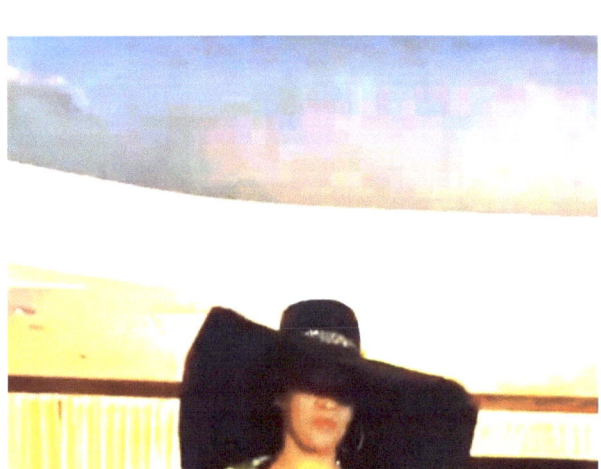
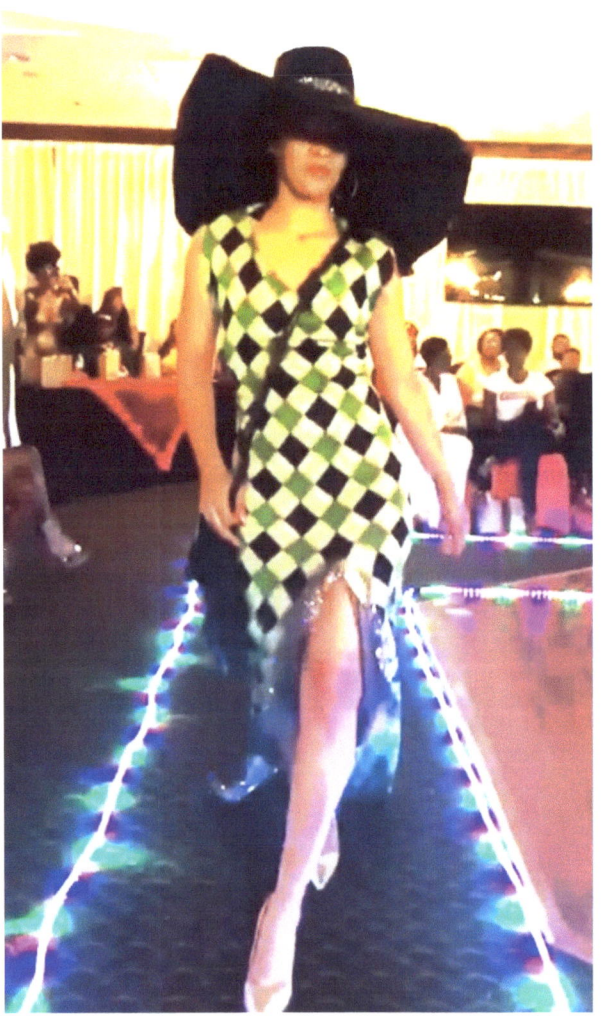
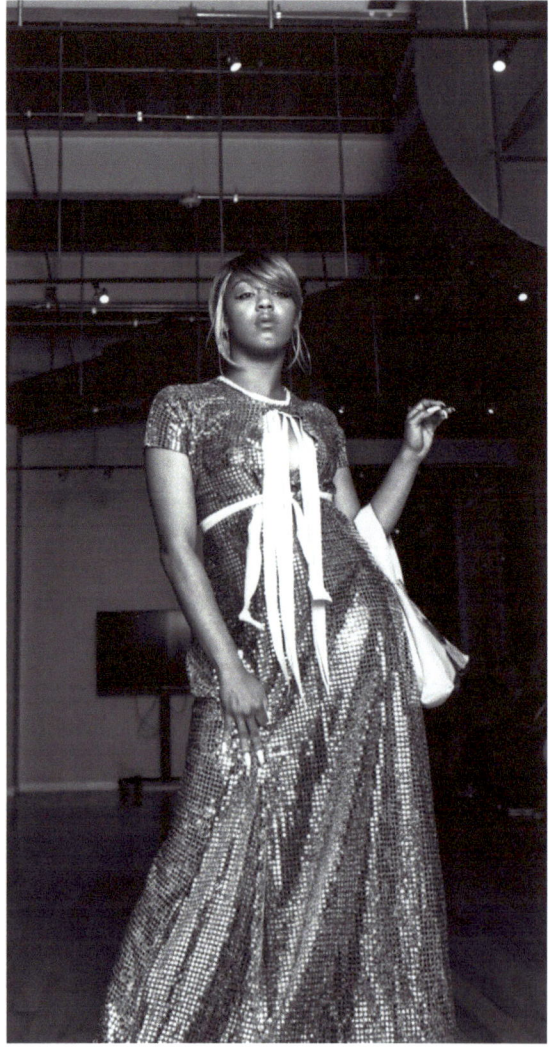

DEE DEE WALKER

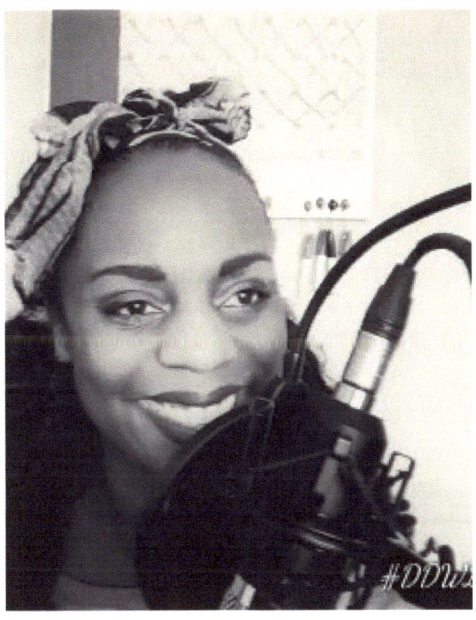

Dee Dee Walker was born in the Bronx, New York. She spent her earlier years growing up in the city, then relocated to Greensboro, North Carolina in her early twenties. She always had a dream of becoming an Actress, after moving to Greensboro she did commercials and landed a spot on Blog Talk Radio.

Walker is currently doing, 'The One and Only Dee Dee Walker Show" on 106TbcRadio.com for the last three years. She has also done video Shows featuring live guests with her Mom for TV, called "Coffee Time" The Big Chat.

Walker has also published an action adventure-thriller screenplay called, ''A Matter of Time'' and wrote episodes of "The Carson's".

She also shares that she has been in Plays and written some scripts along her journey into the exciting world of film. She was cast as the character Portia Love in the recent film, "Butter" which premiered in Greensboro.

"I didn't know where it was going, I just enjoyed being on the set!" She reminisced.

Walker also mentions the short film "The Repast" in which she starred. "I played a Gold Digger! I played a snooty character named Gretchen who used a couple of people. I just love the character; you'll be seeing more of her as there is ongoing interest in her." Her company also filmed and edited the film project.

I asked if she though the recent protests sparked most recently by the murder of George Floyd would lead to police reform, and she like others remains

hopeful that needed changes will come sooner than later.

VANESSA FERGUSON

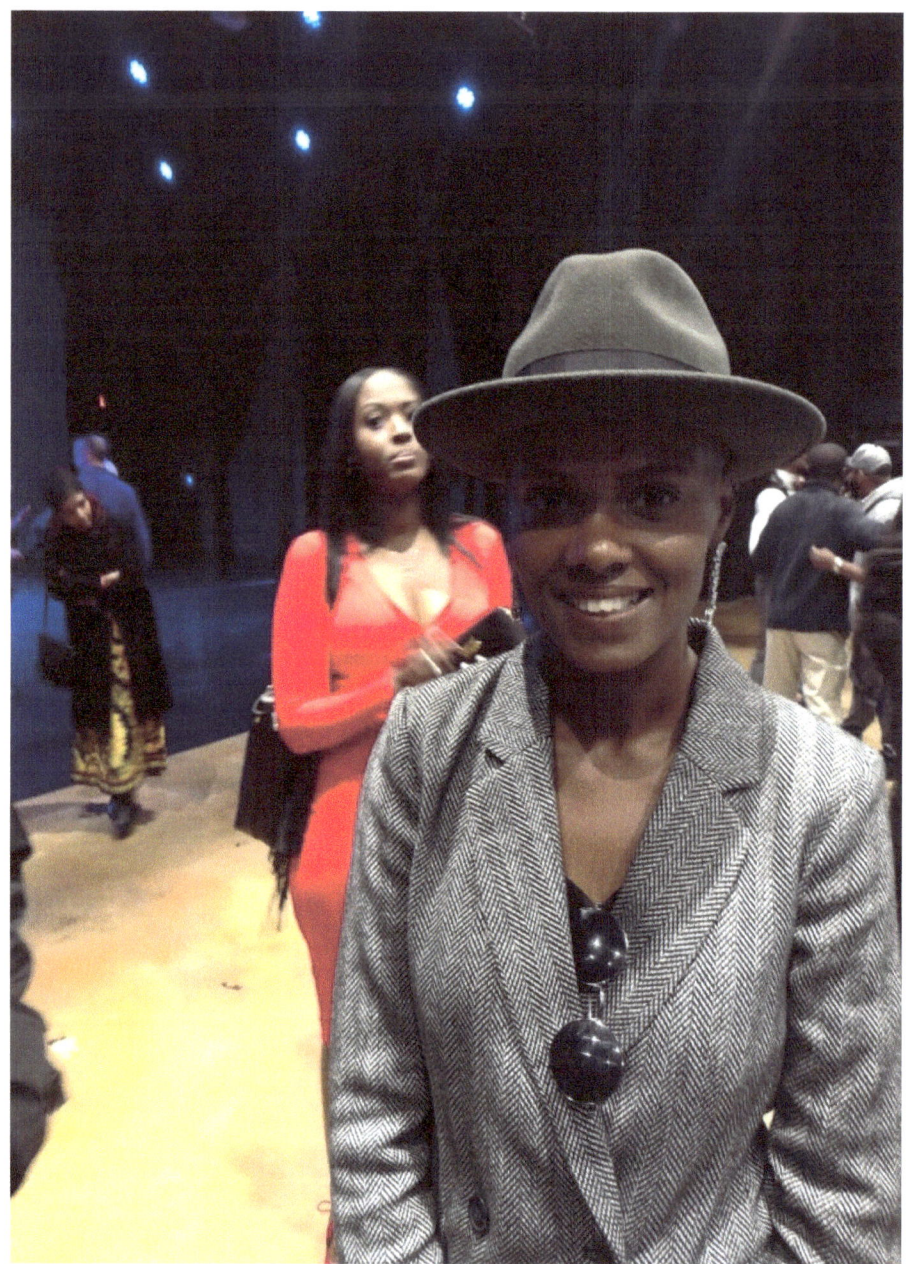

By Fred Little

After being viewed and discovered by millions in 2017 on the global television show "The Voice",

Songstress Vanessa Ferguson keeps creating inspirational songs for music followers.

"I aspire to inspire my fans and my younger fans do the same for me," said Ferguson from her home in North Carolina.

When a reporter first wrote stories about Ferguson she was performing in front of 75 to 200 patrons,

that was prior to "The Voice" television show.

Now she has traveled and thrilled crowds in Italy, Spain, Portugal, Greece, Turkey, and China where her crowds numbered in the thousands.

The Brooklyn born and Greensboro bred Ferguson has opened up for some top acts in music including

Morris Day and The Time, Music Soul Child, Carl Thomas, Mint Condition and the B.B. King All Star Band to name a few.

Vanessa Ferguson's music is layered and complex

"with you" is smooth slow melody that can be heard on the radio.

In contrast, on the edgier side is…"Cries to the Heavens" which deals with police brutality and a Mother losing a child.

By the way look for Ferguson in a documentary on world-famous Jazz Singer Nina Simone.

Ferguson charitably performed in Nina Simone's

house in Charlotte that is being renovated.

DENNIS COFFEY

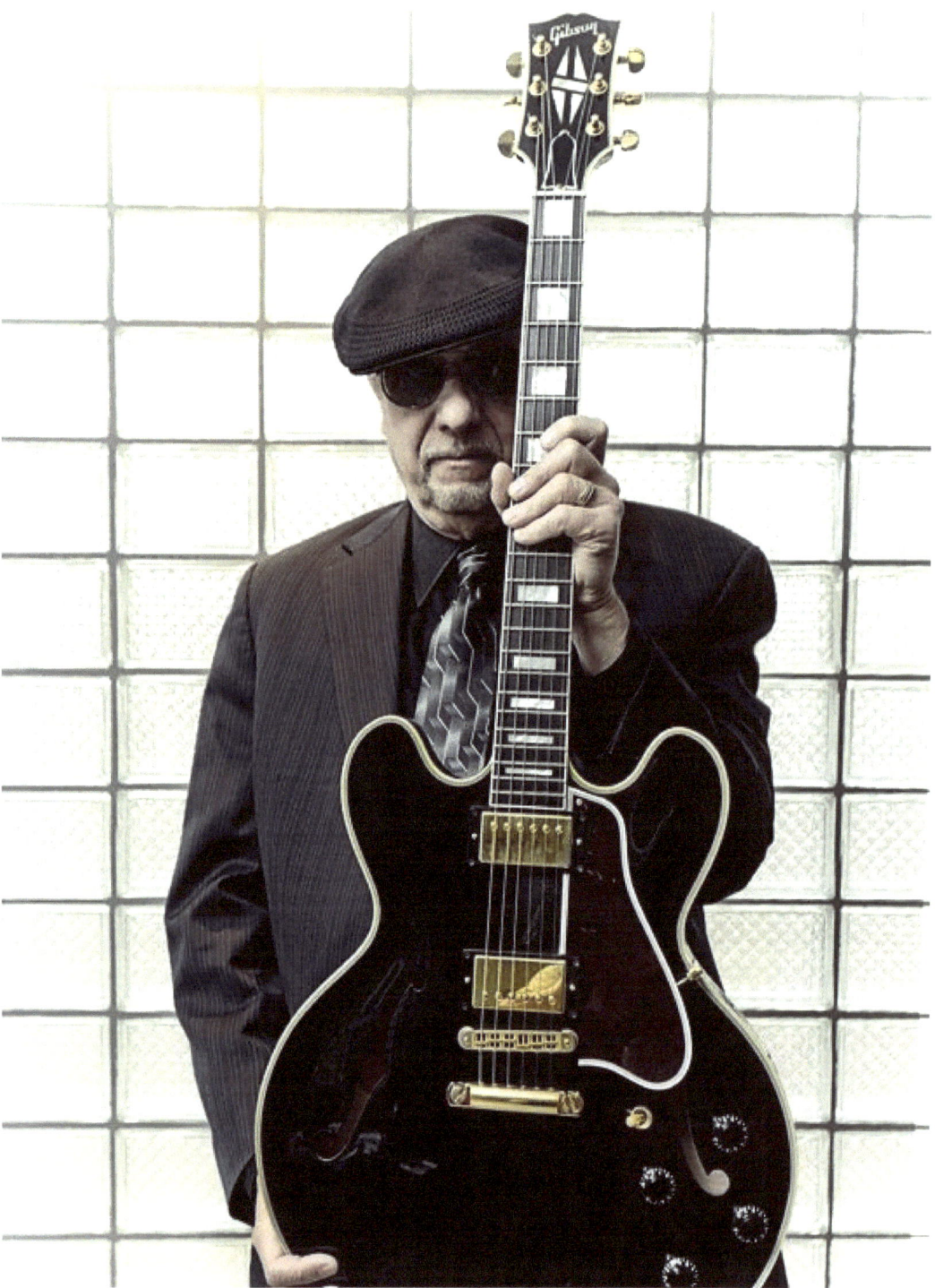

Hi Emmett. I first began studying guitar at the age of 12. My cousins Jim and Marilyn Thompson who lived in Copper City Michigan were playing guitars and showed me a few songs and when I went back to Detroit, I began studying the guitar.

I did my first record date and took two guitar solos at the age of 15. You can find the record on YouTube. It is called **"I'm Gone" by Vic Gallon**.

My advice to beginning musicians is practice, practice and practice some more. I used to practice eight hours a day when I was on summer break from school. The next thing is to join a band and play for people. I was playing a show every Friday and Saturday at the age of 16. I was also a harmony and theory major at **Wayne State University** and learned how to sight read and write music.

I liked **Chuck Berry, BB King and Wes Montgomery**. I got to know Wes and went to hear him when he was playing in Detroit.

At Motown we recorded tracks every day for all the artists. The arrangers and producers were the only ones with us on the sessions.

Our job at **Motown** was to walk in the studio, play an arrangement we never saw before, record one song an hour without any mistakes and make hit records. We did that all day long. **The Funk Brothers** worked together as a team to make great records. We were also friends. One thing I remember is when I was doing sessions at Motown every day in LA, I got a call from them to play with the **Jackson Five** at a show. I asked when the rehearsal was. (I had just gone to a rehearsal with **Barbara Streisand** and a 60 piece orchestra for an upcoming show with her). They told me the guitar player quit or got fired at the rehearsal so I would have to do the show without a rehearsal. **The Jackson Five included both Michael and Janet.** Motown reminded me they were paying me union scale and one half for every session I did in LA so I had to do this. I played the show without the rehearsal and it was a great!

I was writing orchestral charts along with Mike Theodore and one day I wondered what it would sound like if I wrote horn and string like parts for guitars. I wrote ten songs and Mike and I produced the session. I learned how to use breakdowns from Motown producer **Norman Whitfield.** I just broke the song down and **Bob Babbitt** came up with this incredible bass solo. I also had funk brothers **Eddie Bongo Brown** on congas, Jack Ashford on tambourine, Uriel Jones and Pistol Allen on drums and I played guitar. I also overdubbed nine guitars on the melody as the **Detroit Guitar Band**. I had Funk Brother **Earl Van Dyke** on piano on **Scorpio**.

Most musicians in Metro Detroit are out of work because our Governor closed the restaurants and bars. I wrote and recorded the main theme and love theme for the film **Black Belt Jones** for **Warner Brothers** when I lived in LA. My latest CD out is "**Down by the River**" on the Detroit Music Factory/Mack Avenue Records. I decided to leave that label and am looking for a new record label who will support what I do.

Dennis Coffey

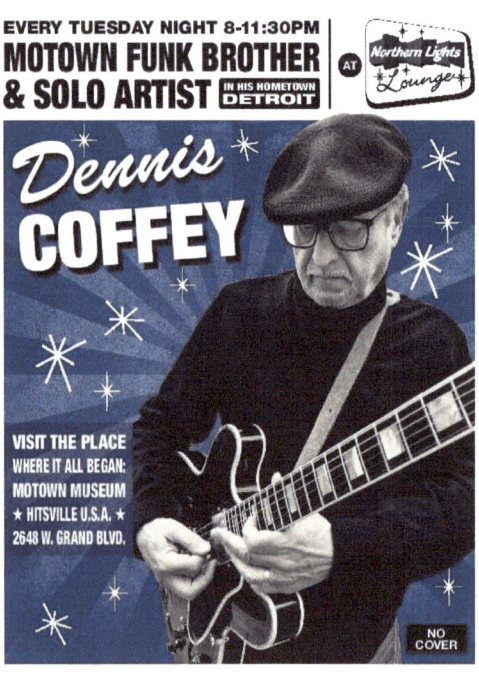

EMMETT WILLIAMS

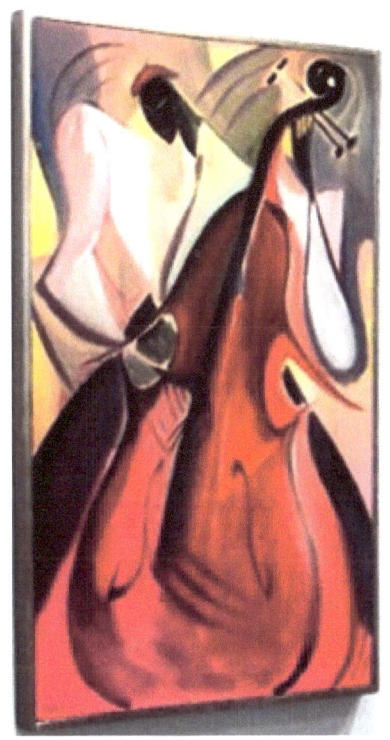 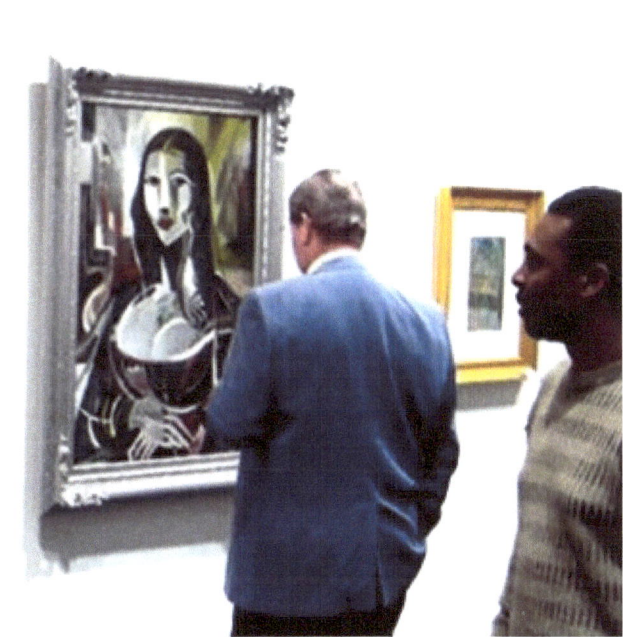

The Greenville Museum of Art

Living Artists of North Carolina Exhibition

This was one of my most favorite Group Exhibitions in March 2008 and the last one me and my good friend Floyd Newkirk did before he passed away. The atmosphere was electric and we had a very nice after-party at the Starlight Café.

The entire exhibit was amazing and nothing but good things were said about it. Newkirk and me met at Greensboro, North Carolina's African-American Atelier after I became a member. We hung shows and did some mural projects in the city as well as exhibited our Jazz paintings together.

The day I saw his Coltrane painting, I knew I would own it and a few other of his works eventually.

We drank a couple of times a week for about 4 years.

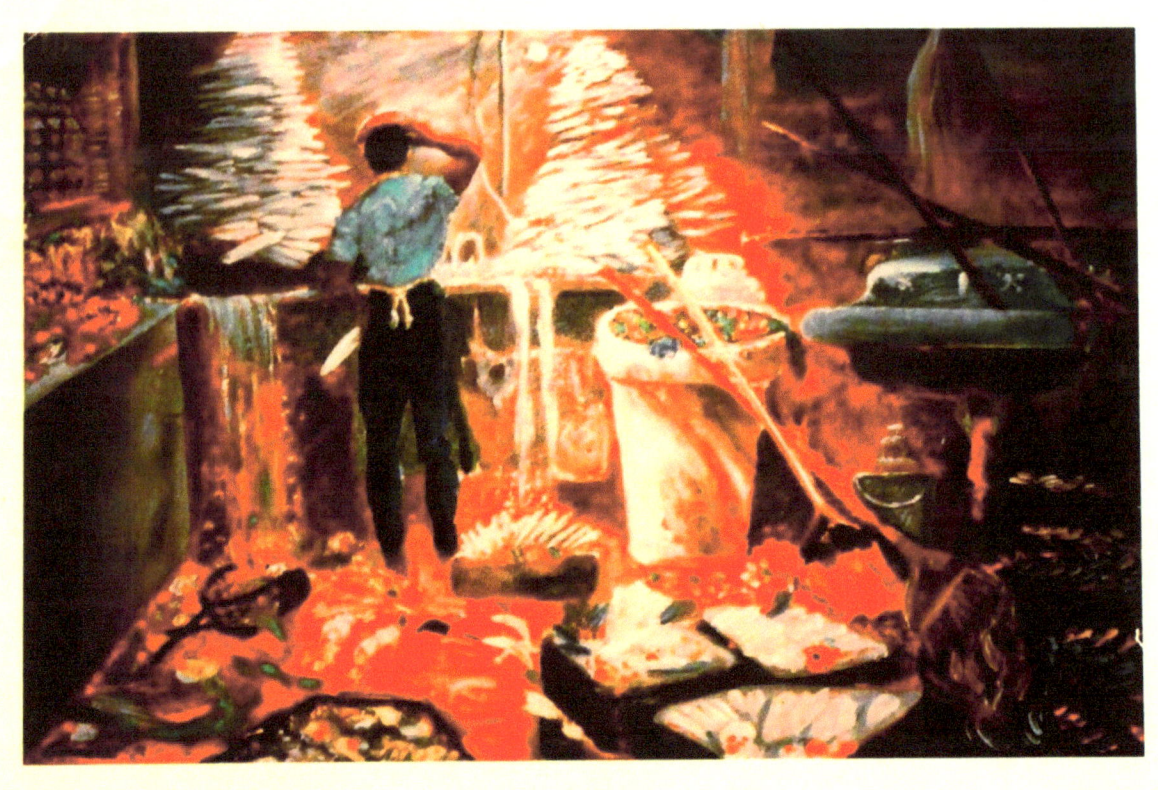

This is me as a Dishwasher around age 22. Dreaming of the day my works would hang in a museum. By age 24 while working as a mail-clerk I was given a challenge to organize a Staff/Volunteer Art exhibition at The National Museum for Women.

Two years later The Dishwasher study hung on a boardroom wall in a Museum.

Then in a downtown DC gallery called The Pavilion Gallery where it sold.

I still hadn't had a Solo, until around the time the Van Gogh exhibition happened. I did my best to get coverage and eventually after being denied by almost everyone, I started challenging the press to go and see the show before they said no.

"Go see it, and if it's not worth writing about, just keep writing about Van Gogh."

Writer Herb Quarles of The Afro-American Newspapers in DC went. Then became a fan and wrote a story following up with more coverage.

Things got kinda tough as rents were out of control. I had two jobs and was about to get a third when the rest of my family said they were going to relocate to North Carolina.

There was nothing keeping me, as even the new gallery drew a line where they wouldn't cross pricewise. I will never understand it.

If a Ferrari is painted Black it's still a Ferrari isn't it? And the value does not go down because of its color, whether it is applied to Artists like Basquiat or me.

If you don't ask for what you believe you're work is worth or the Artists you are representing how can you get it? Also you don't need to ask, just state the price and don't blink. Wait for the right buyer to come and get it.

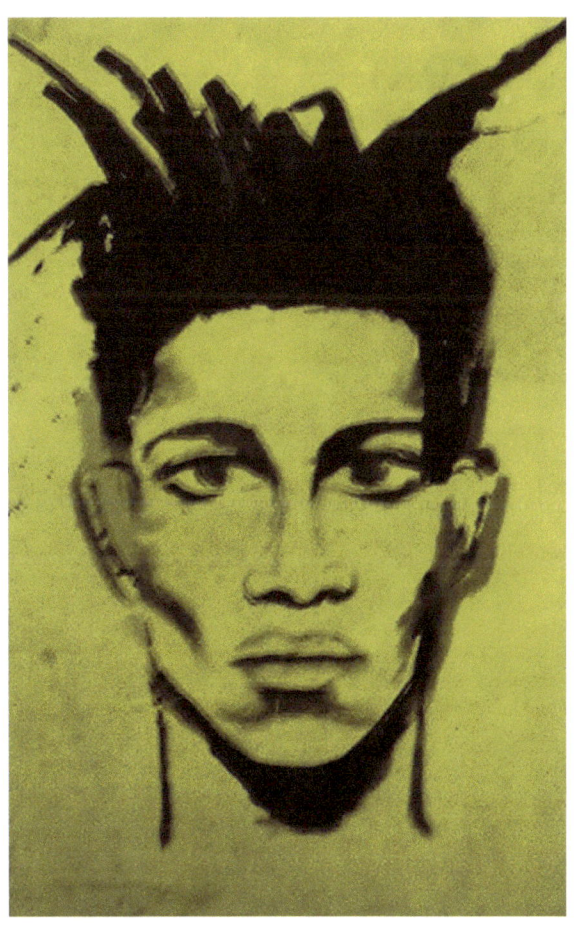

I did this sketch of Basquiat after I met him in the '80s.

I could tell he was a painter, but had only recognized him from a music video.

A friend I was with told me he was an Abstractionist, and I was already annoyed with the focus on that in my classes, being a figure painter.

Later in life I read a book on him and saw more of his work and was extremely impressed especially on learning we liked painting to some of the same Jazz recordings.

So maybe it's time to show some more images and briefly touch on them. The genre of Jazz opened a lot of doors for me as I did mural works and sold originals to all the owners of Takoma Station Tavern in DC.

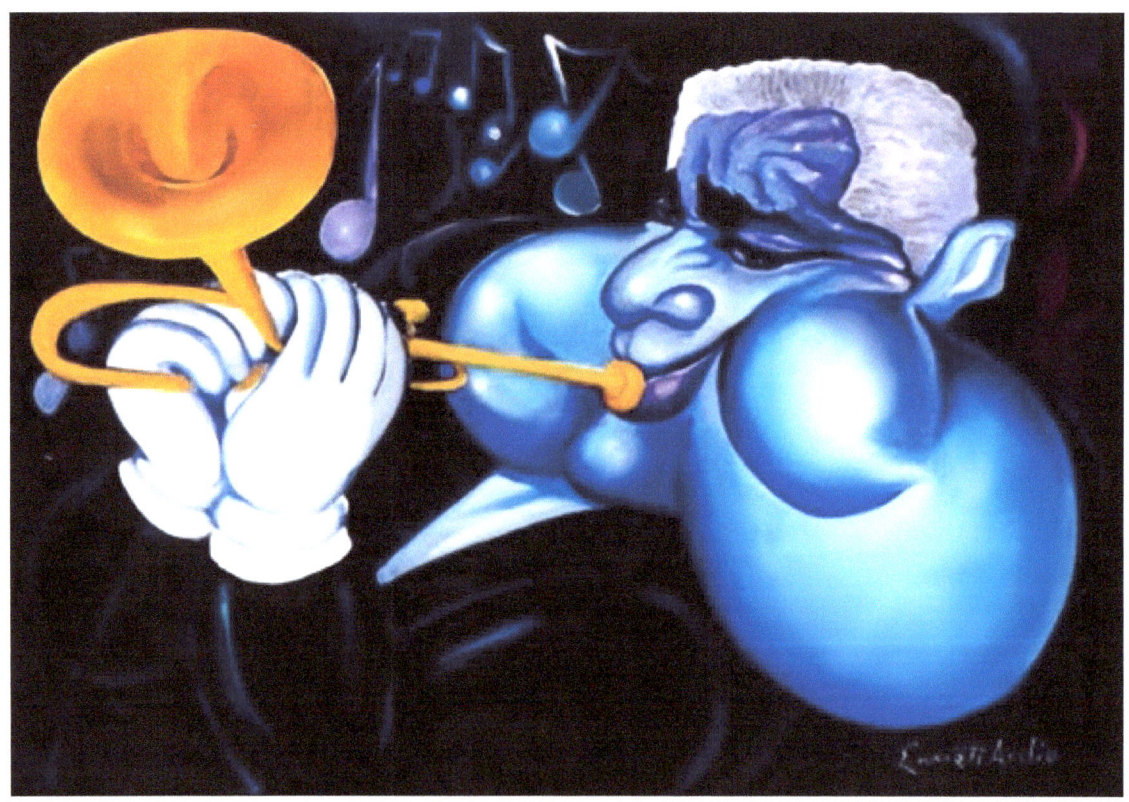

Around this time in 1997 I was still painting in oils; I just wouldn't show them until they were dry, which took forever. By the time somebody saw a wet oil painting and it dried, they'd spent the money on something else.

'Dizzy-Blue' pictured above I held onto for as long as possible. It almost got sold at Takoma Station until the gallery saw it.

Oils are hard to shoot, but I managed a few good shots before film became obsolete.

So there was demand for the Jazz works, oil paintings and surrealism so I just combined the elements. Then I did them in Acrylics, and changed my style to something faster. The Dizzy was about four weeks or so to dry.

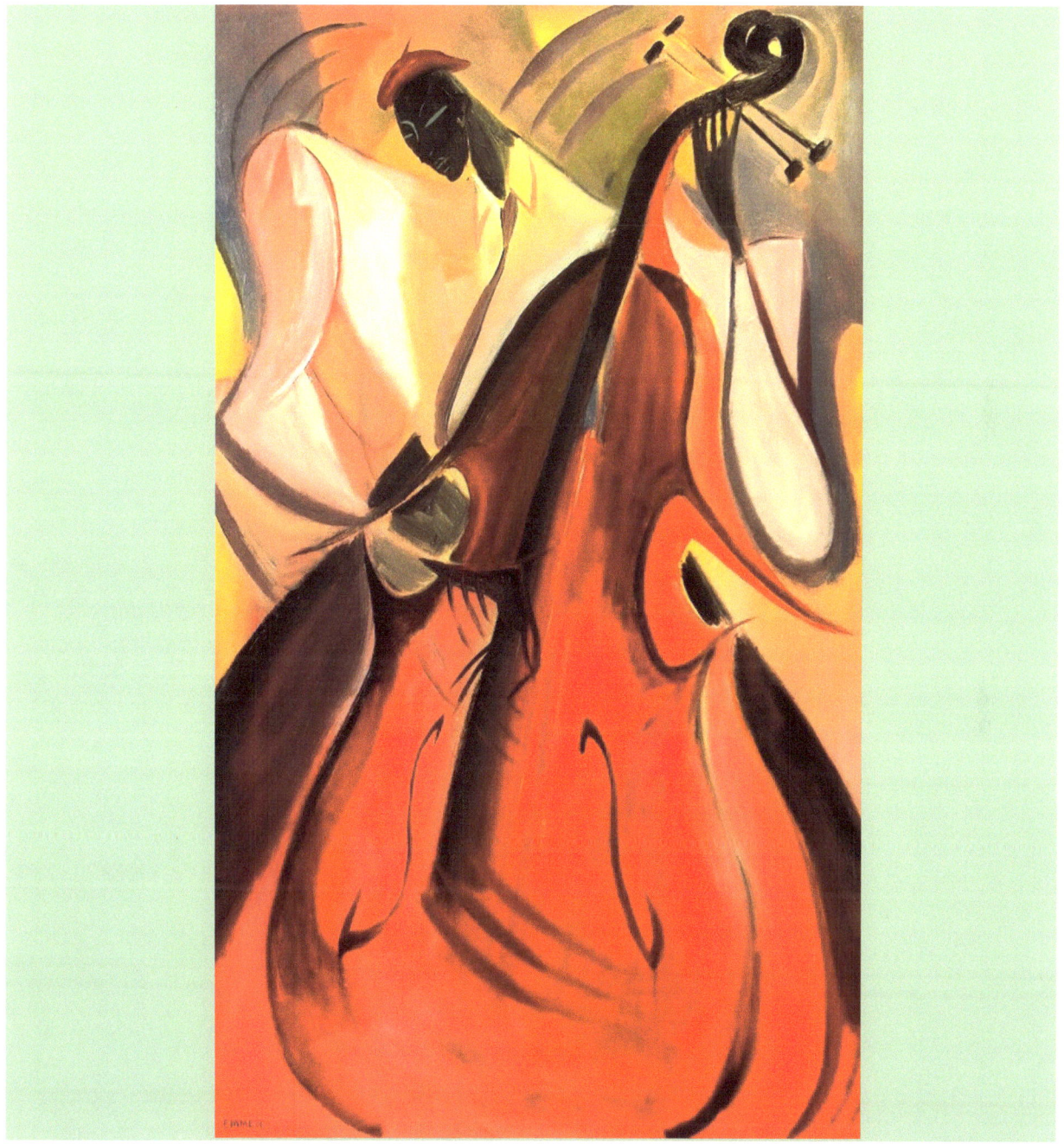

I need my work done in one day. So if it's an oil painting, it's just a month to dry. Experiment number one was the Bass Player. A sketch of a live subject at Greensboro's Festival of Lights at the Kress building, after I sketched him I went back to my freezing studio and started an oil painting.

My linseed oil froze in my one good brush as I worked. I switched to linseed only as a thinner as turpentine kept me in migraine headaches, eventually I had to stop using it too however. When I painted I was in a perpetual state of dizziness due to fumes, when I switched to acrylics, my health and my palette improved, the drying time forced me to work quicker as well. So The Bass Player painting was one of the last pieces in oil. I only touched it again to sign it neatly.

I painted it in a place I'd seen with my boss as we sat in traffic. He offered to get it for me if I guaranteed to make a certain amount of money a day. I told him "If I ever decided I wanted that building I could take it all by myself."

And a year later proved it.

My works then began appearing in publications in Greensboro, North Carolina. I became friends with most of the writers. We did some drinking.

I met execs at all levels, and most find my businesslike demeanor amusing.

I am not asking permission to be what I want to be. I'm a CEO whether I call myself one or not. I conceive, design, manufacture and market, process sales and budget the profits like any other business. I will never go out of business, or fail because I am the business and the brand.

My work and concepts will improve and then I'll expand them into the stratosphere.

As creative's, people have perceptions of what art and Artists are about. Buyers need to be informed about the product we need to sell.

Press coverage is a wonderful thing, but you can't depend on it. You can depend on branding yourself/work so well that it precedes you and the buyers come looking for you directly. That is goal one.

This becomes the point of self-determination.

Repeatable sales success comes from educated consumers who are constantly made aware of what is available from you and worth them seeking you out for it.

It is for this reason that creative's sellers need to create consistent tools like publications, that don't just vomit out nonsensical dribble nobody cares about.

Focus on why your product is important, why you make it, how much it is etc.

Things that matter, not just chatter.

Contact Information:

EMMETT WILLIAMS

PUBLISHER@EMMETTMAGAZINE.COM

352-244-9999

© EMMETTMAGAZINE.COM 2020

www.ingramcontent.com/pod-product-compliance
Lightning Source LLC
Chambersburg PA
CBHW040454220526
45473CB00004B/1635